INTERVIEWING
Its Principles and Methods

Annette Garrett

INTERVIEWING
Its Principles and Methods

Third edition, revised by

Margaret M. Mangold and Elinor P. Zaki

Family Service Association of America
New York

Copyright © 1982 by
Family Service Association of America
44 East 23rd Street, New York, N.Y. 10010

First edition copyright © 1942, 1970, second edition
copyright © 1972, by
Family Service Association of America

Garrett, Annette.
   Interviewing, its principles and methods.
   1. Interviewing.   I. Zaki, Elinor P.   II. Mangold,
Margaret M.   III. Title.
HV41.G34   1982   361.3′22   82-1591
ISBN 0-87304-195-X   AACR2
ISBN 0-87304-194-1 (pbk.)

Printed in the United States of America

Contents

Foreword

When *Interviewing: Its Principles and Methods* was first published in 1942, social work professionals hailed it as a seminal work. It quickly became a basic text and ultimately a classic for schools of social work in the United States and abroad. Translated into twenty foreign languages, published in Braille, and transcribed on phonograph records, it has realized a total sale, in English alone, of more than half a million copies. Its value is recognized not only in social work but in many other professional disciplines: medicine, teaching, and psychology among them. Large business concerns have also discovered the usefulness of *Interviewing* for trainers, supervisors, and administrators.

The special qualities of sound principle and detailed example—presented clearly and gracefully—that Annette Garrett gave to her book are still characteristic of this third revised edition.

Part I's treatment of the nature of interviewing has been thoroughly updated by the edition's co-authors, Margaret M. Mangold and Elinor P. Zaki. Of the sixteen interview chapters that comprise Part II, fifteen are entirely new. Mrs. Mangold and Mrs. Zaki provide analysis and comment for each interview to show how the principles and methods of professional interviewing are applied in them.

Mrs. Mangold and Mrs. Zaki were co-authors of the second revised edition of *Interviewing*, which was published in 1972. Their writing reflects their wide and rich experience as caseworkers, supervisors, teachers, consultants to non-social work organizations, writers, and editors.

Mrs. Mangold, after receiving an A.M. degree from the University of Chicago School of Social Service Administration, was a caseworker in the Family Service Bureau of United Charities of Chicago. Later, she joined the staff of the Charity Organization Society (now the Community Service Society) in New York as a caseworker and student supervisor. While there, she was "loaned" to a New York City elementary public school to demonstrate the services of a school social worker, an assignment which led to the school's employment of a permanent social worker. During World War II, her agency arranged for her to train volunteers in the New York City office of Army Emergency Relief and, with the part-time assistance of two student social workers, to provide professional services to wives of enlisted men. Following this experience, she became case supervisor and later executive director of Staten Island Social Service, a family agency. Later, she returned to practice as a psychiatric social worker and student supervisor at the Adelphi University Mental Health Clinic in Garden City, New York. This period was followed by several years as associate professor in the School of Social Work at Adelphi University. Her career led her next to Family Service Association of America (FSAA), where she became director of publications service and editor of *Social Casework*.

Mrs. Zaki began her social work career in the family agency in Lansing, Michigan. After graduating from the New York School of Social Work, she joined the staff of the Charity Organization Society in New York City. Mrs. Zaki then worked as consultant and caseworker for two day nurseries in New York City. Later, she was employed on a part-time basis by three family agencies in Westchester County, New York. When her husband was assigned by his government to be dean of the recently established first school of social work in Cairo, Egypt, Mrs. Zaki accompanied him and introduced and taught casework courses in the new school. After returning to the United States, she worked as a casework supervisor with the Family Service Association of Dayton, Ohio, before joining FSAA in New York. She preceded Mrs. Mangold as publications director and editor of *Social Casework*.

In their separate and their joint years at FSAA, Mrs. Zaki and Mrs. Mangold edited and published numerous books, pamphlets, and teaching records, as well as articles for *Social Casework*. They served on the Committee for Teaching Materials of the Council on Social Work Education and the Committee on Ethics of the New York City Chapter of the National Association of Social Workers. Mrs. Zaki was a member of the Publications Committee of the National Conference on Social Welfare and was an alumni representative on the Advisory Council of the Columbia University School of Social Work.

Robert A. Elfers
Director, Publications Service
Family Service Association
of America

Acknowledgments

I t is not an exercise in editorial hyperbole to state that without the enthusiastic encouragement, sustained interest, and investment of much thought and time of the following persons, this revision would not have been possible. We are warmly appreciative of the colleagues who were our consultants and contributors of the illustrative interviews. They are:

Terri Brannen, student social worker at the time the case material was selected, Department of Social Work, The New York Hospital, New York, New York.

Marjorie A. Jonas, director, Department of Social Work, The New York Hospital, New York, New York.

Michael Ladner, at the time interviews were chosen, student social worker, Personal Service Unit, District Council 37, American Federation of State, County and Municipal Employees AFL-CIO, New York, New York.

Anthony Mazzella, supervisor, Personal Service Unit, District Council 37, American Federation of State, County and Municipal Employees AFL-CIO, New York, New York.

Lynn Pearlmutter, social worker, Family Service Society, New Orleans, Louisiana.

Mary Ann Salerno, social worker, Department of Social Work, The New York Hospital, New York, New York.

John W. Taylor, social worker, Family Service Association of Orange County, Tustin, California.

Alice Ullmann, associate director, Department of Social Work, The New York Hospital, New York, New York.

Vincent Vaccaro, Ph.D., psychologist, Employee Counseling Programs, Jewish Board of Family and Children's Services, New York, New York.

Florence W. Vigilante, D.S.W., associate professor,
Hunter College School of Social Work, Hunter College of the
City University, New York, New York.

Esther Wald, coordinator of clinical services, Family Service of South Lake County, Highland Park, Illinois.

Barbara Ziff-Ratner, at the time the case material was
selected, outreach worker, Jewish Family and Children's Service, Pittsburgh, Pennsylvania.

We are also indebted to two staff members of the FSAA
Publications Service: Dianne Walber for her service as copy
and production editor and Eleanore Wamp, administrative
secretary, who so graciously and cheerfully assumed responsibility for the many chores related to this project. Miss
Wamp's attention to all details of the considerable correspon-
dence and her patience in providing and supervising the typing
and proofreading of several drafts are greatly appreciated.

M.M.M.

E.P.Z.

Introduction

In undertaking this revision of the internationally acclaimed *Interviewing* by Annette Garrett, our intent has been to illustrate some of the new and developing areas of current casework practice and, by including more than one interview, enable the reader to study the on-going treatment process. In some examples, a summary of the results of treatment is also given.

With the generous assistance of colleagues across the country, we obtained examples of the kinds of problems being brought to social workers today. It is a wide range: from problems that have been of concern to social workers for many years—parent-child relationships, marital conflicts, problems of the aged, and problems related to illness and death—to newer areas of service in cases of domestic violence, special needs of remarried families, and industrial social work.

The treatment of violent behavior within the family is presented in two chapters of potential and actual child abuse (the latter is the only chapter retained from the previous editions) and three interviews involving abusive husbands. These portray a caseworker's use of specific techniques to teach management of anger and handling of stress. The worker's interviewing activity and interventions vary, as seen in a first interview with a young husband under court order to accept counseling, an interview with a married couple midway through treatment, and one with a young man, separated from his wife, nearing termination of treatment.

Similarly, another chapter presents three interviews from

the beginning, middle, and ending phases of treatment which illustrate casework with an adolescent girl struggling to emancipate herself from a destructive home situation.

Two chapters present examples of interviews with remarried families. The cases were selected to illustrate both the preventive and remedial help needed in these increasingly common family situations. More stepparents now openly recognize the problems in familial relationships and seek counseling from family agencies. The opportunity for preventive help is effectively shown in the response of one couple, with young children, married only two months when the wife applied to the family agency for help in preserving her marriage. In contrast, the second couple had been married for six years when unresolved feelings related to the wife's first marriage and divorce surfaced as her older son entered adolescence.

The growing field of industrial social work is attested to by the offerings of special courses and fieldwork placements in graduate schools of social work. Increasingly, students are selecting it as a specialization in preparation for on-going professional practice. Two chapters relate to this area of practice. In one, counseling is provided under union auspices and in the other, counseling is made available in a family agency with the fee paid by the employer as arranged in a contract between the corporation and the agency.

The effectiveness of family interviews is well illustrated in four chapters as is the use of joint interviews in other chapters.

The counselors whose work is presented in this book represent a range of experience from graduate students to those with graduate degrees—highly skilled counselors with many years in professional practice. The sequence of chapters in Part II relates chiefly to the years of professional practice and resultant expertise.

Margaret M. Mangold
Elinor P. Zaki

PART I
The Nature
Of Interviewing

1 Interviewing as an art

Everyone engages in interviewing. Sometimes he interviews; sometimes he is interviewed.* The mother interviews the principal of the school in which she is thinking of entering her son. The principal, in turn, interviews the mother and the boy. A young woman is interviewed by her prospective employer and, in turn, interviews the employer. Some people, because of the nature of their work, spend a good deal of time in interviewing. The attendant in an information booth devotes all of his working hours to miniature interviews. Lawyers, doctors, nurses, newspaper reporters, police officers, the clergy, counselors, credit personnel, personnel managers, employers, all devote a considerable amount of time to talking with people, getting information from them, advising them, helping them. They acquire various degrees of skill in the art of interviewing, sometimes consciously, usually unconsciously.

Social caseworkers are interviewers par excellence. Their tasks make them professional interviewers. For some of them interviewing becomes an art and, indeed, almost a science. These professional interviewers have been able to formulate and organize the basic principles of interviewing into the beginnings of a systematic body of knowledge.

Probably everyone starting to interview wishes there was a list of rules to follow. Unfortunately, however, it is impossible to enumerate a complete list of infallible rules for all interviewing, or even for any particular kind. Interviewing takes place between human beings, and people are too individual to be reduced to a formula.

*The masculine pronoun is used with neuter nouns throughout this book as a matter of convenience. Its use is not to be interpreted as having a sexist connotation.

To be sure, there are certain psychological traits that characterize most people most of the time, and a skilled interviewer will do well to keep some of the more important ones in mind. There are characteristic modes of human action and reaction, and awareness of them tends to increase the satisfactoriness of one's relationship with others. Interviewing involves a closer and subtler relation between human beings than initially may be recognized, and skill in conducting this relationship can be increased through knowledge of the fundamental factors involved.

Some people fear that a self-conscious study of the principles of interviewing may detract from the warm friendliness and real interest in other individuals that are so essential for the successful practice of the art. Certainly there is no necessity for warmth and friendliness to disappear with knowledge. An informed person need not be unfriendly. One need not be ignorant of human psychology to love human beings. Indeed, the opposite is often true. There are few things so frustrating as to love someone but not know how to give the help he desperately needs; on the contrary, to be able to help those we love increases our affection for them.

Sometimes, warm human interest does vanish from interviewing, and when that happens it becomes a monotonous, mechanical function that is relatively valueless. But the cause of this kind of interviewing, when it occurs, is not knowledge of the rich interplay of one human mind with another, but the ignorance that regards interviewing as a routine affair of asking set questions and recording answers. Interviewing is indeed far more than a routine procedure. With a proper understanding of even some of the intricacies of human personality and of the effective give-and-take between two complex human beings, our attention and warm interest are aroused in increasing measure, and the interviewing process becomes anything but routine.

Interviewing is an art, a skilled technique that can be improved and eventually perfected primarily through continued practice. But practice alone is not enough. Skills can be developed to their fullest only when practice is accompanied by knowledge about interviewing and conscious study of one's own practice. Knowledge of the theory underlying interviewing gives us certain material in the light of which we can critically examine our present techniques and discern ways in which they can be improved.

The obvious fact about interviewing is that it involves communication between two people. It might be called professional conversation. Special problems confront both interviewer and interviewee. We begin to obtain some notion of the complexities involved if we recall some of the feelings we have had while on the way to be interviewed. Perhaps we were seeking to borrow money, were consulting a doctor or a lawyer, or were applying for a job. We may have felt some fear at the prospect of talking with an unknown person and of revealing our needs to him. We may have been uncertain as to what we might have to tell, fearful that the interviewer might wish to know more than we were willing to reveal, might not understand us, or might not grant our request.

On the other hand, when we first began to interview, what were some of the worries that plagued us? We wondered whether we would say the right things to put our client at ease. Would we not be able to draw him out? What would we do if he did not talk, and if he did, would we be able to recognize and select the significant facts in his remarks and behavior?

For an interview to be successful, the diverse fears of both interviewer and interviewee must be allayed, and the diverse desires of both must be met. Rapport must be established between the two, a relationship that will enable the interviewee to reveal the essential facts of his situation and that will enable the interviewer to be most effective in helping him.

To give meaning and background to the suggestions for interviewing that we make later and to enable the interviewer to carry out these suggestions with understanding, we shall devote the next chapter to a study of certain basic facts about human nature, concentrating on those that are most significant for interviewing. The following comments indicate the special areas that will be discussed in some detail.

Although most of us feel the need at times for expert legal or medical knowledge, we tend to feel that we already possess an adequate working knowledge of the nature of human beings and their behavior. Such knowledge, however, is likely to be a combination of old wives' tales and generalizations based on necessarily limited personal experience and distorted by personal prejudices. We interpret others in relation to ourselves, forgetting that our view is influenced by a host of more or less concealed prejudices and emotions.

Interviewers should have more than a casual knowledge of the important role in human motivation of influences other than the conscious and the rational. They should apply this knowledge, not only to an understanding of their clients' personalities, needs, prejudices, and emotions, but also to an understanding of their own. The wise maxim of the ancient Greeks, "Know thyself," applies especially to interviewers.

An interviewer's attention must continuously be directed in two ways: toward himself as well as toward his client. Sometimes this need for two-way direction makes him fear that he may become overly self-conscious in his responses and lose so much of his natural human warmth that his client will be alienated. But, he soon learns the contrary danger—that spontaneous and unselfconscious response may be recognized by the client as only a surface response supported by such insufficient understanding of his real feelings that effective help will be impossible.

Another chapter is devoted to a discussion of the purposes of interviews, which take place for all sorts of reasons. At one end of the scale is the interview of the census taker, whose immediate purpose simply is to obtain specific information. At the opposite end is the therapeutic interviewing of the psychiatrist or psychoanalyst. Between these two extremes lie the vast majority of interviews, the aim of which is to help in one way or another, and information is sought primarily to direct this help to actual needs and to make it effective.

It is impossible to discuss interviewing in a vacuum. The specific techniques of interviewing vary with the purpose in mind. Because nearly all interviews involve the obtaining of information for the purpose of helping people, we use as typical examples interviews of this kind on a professional level, interviews characteristic of general social casework. This kind of interviewing furnishes rich material for a discussion of the nature and methods of the art. Another advantage of choosing this general field is that applications to specific fields of interviewing can be made readily.

Because we approach interviewing from its use in general casework practice, it is inevitable that some discussion of basic casework concepts will be included. But insofar as possible, our attention will be focused on interviewing per se. We shall avoid discussing casework concepts as such because casework deserves a much more comprehensive treatment than would be possible here.

The general discussion of the methods and techniques of interviewing, although illustrated at each point, is supplemented by a section giving a number of interviews in more detail. These illustrations also provide useful source material on which the experienced interviewer may wish to test his own procedures.

It should be clear that the discussion presented here gives but a selection of some of the most salient features of interviewing. They have been culled from a vast store of relevant knowledge accumulated over the years by professional workers in the casework field. Again, it should be noted that there is nothing sacrosanct in the order in which the various topics are treated. They are so interrelated that a discussion of any one of them involves some aspects of many of the others. In practice, things have to be said in a linear order rather than all at once, but it might be well to remember that an understanding of some of the topics treated later will help toward understanding the subjects discussed first.

2 Understanding human nature

There are certain basic facts about the nature of human beings with which every interviewer should be familiar. The different motives of interviewers will lead to different uses of such knowledge. The saleswoman, dominated by the profit motive, will use her knowledge of human psychology to increase her sales; the propagandist, whether his motives are good or bad, will use his knowledge to increase the infectiousness of his ideas. It is assumed that the readers of this book will be motivated by the desire to be of service to their fellow human beings and will use their knowledge of human nature to that end.

Human Motivation

The reasons underlying some forms of human behavior are clear both to the actor and to outside observers. Sometimes they are concealed from outsiders but are recognized more or less clearly by the actor. Sometimes they are unknown even to him. For example, a man applying for a job insults his prospective employer. How can such behavior be understood? Did he not know he was being insulting? Or, did he not know that an insult would prevent his being hired? Or, did he not really want the job? Or what? In seeking to explain his failure to get the job, he might say, "The foreman was unreasonable." But very likely he would himself be aware of the unsatisfactoriness of such an explanation. Often people who behave in some such irrational way are as much puzzled by their behavior as is anyone else.

We can sympathize more readily with such a person's bewilderment if we realize that there is much of our own behavior that we find hard to explain. Our glib rationalizations do not satisfy even ourselves. Why do we sometimes fly into a rage if we are kept waiting for a minute, when at other times we are willing to wait in line fairly patiently for half an hour? Why do we sometimes punish a child severely for a slight fault and at other times let flagrant misbehavior go unremarked? Why do some people in particular "bug" us?

If we knew all, we would doubtless understand all. Bizarre behavior, like more usual behavior, has its causes, but sometimes they are deeply hidden. In dealing with others it is seldom possible or essential to understand fully the causes of their actions. It is essential, however, to realize that their behavior is motivated. Its source may lie in the depths of their personalities where neither they nor we can readily discover it. In a complex personality, with its many interconnected causal chains, the factors underlying a given bit of behavior are usually many and varied. A single cause cannot be isolated, and to attempt to force the individual to name one is to demand the impossible. He will be forced to resort to an inadequate rationalization.

The recognition that much human motivation is unconscious will enable the interviewer to be more tolerant, less condemnatory, and thus better able to help his client effectively. Instead of becoming impatient with rationalizations, he will realize that the motives that the client disguises even to himself are probably sources of deep and painful anxiety.

Unconscious motivation is much more common than we ordinarily recognize in our attempt to understand people. Too often we look for intellectual *grounds* for behavior rather than for psychological *causes* rooted in feelings and emotions. Drives are emotional in nature, and actions controlled by them have their source in feeling rather than in intellect. A person who apparently likes, but really dislikes, another "forgets" a luncheon engagement with her and in extenuation pleads a busy day. A man fired from a job because of incompetence "explains" that the work was too strenuous for him. Why a client says certain things and leaves others unsaid, why a child with a high I.Q. fails in school, why a wife who effusively protests her love for her husband continually belittles him, are questions whose answers are to be sought not in intellectual but in emotional terms. Explanations such as "He's deceitful," "He's lazy," and "She's just being modest about him" are clearly inadequate.

Yet, for many people such remarks conclude the discussion and block any real understanding.

Objective and Subjective Aspects

Every situation has its objective and subjective aspects. A man loses his job. That is an objective fact. His feelings about this event constitute a subjective reaction. A woman is ill with cancer. That is a medical fact. But every person who has any sort of illness has accompanying it certain feelings about the illness. There are variations in the physical aspects of cancer, but there are also many variations in human reactions to the disease. Thus, we could run the gamut of human experiences and note that every objective experience—marriage, hunger, getting a job, leaving one's children in a day care center—has its accompanying subjective counterpart of emotional attitudes. Experience and skill lead to an increasing awareness of this interrelationship.

Social workers sometimes contrast what they call the reality situation of a client with his emotional problems. This separation is unfortunate because it sometimes leads us to operate as if these two areas were mutually exclusive. The implication is that the emotional components of the situation are not real, whereas, they certainly are real to the person experiencing them. The way one feels about a situation is as much a fact as the situation itself. To avoid such an erroneous implication, we shall discuss the objective aspects and the subjective aspects of a client's situation. Both are always present.

We are directing our attention primarily to subjective aspects, to feelings, attitudes, and emotions, because we recognize that they are as important as the objective facts themselves and are much more likely to be overlooked. Our concentration on them does not imply any lack of appreciation of the significance of the objective facts. We recognize, of course, that too much attention to subjective factors would limit service to the individual just as much as would lack of appreciation of them. In practice we must be extremely vigilant so that we give each group of factors its due weight.

A student who applies for a scholarship because his father has just retired and cannot afford college costs may be even more worried about his father's poor health, which necessitated the retirement, than he is about the financial problem. The dean who notes only the latter may be failing to give the young man the help he most urgently needs or may be giving a scholarship to a student whose anxieties will prevent his profiting from it.

In seeking to help people even in very simple situations, we need to listen not only to their objective requests, but also to the undertones that reveal their feelings and give us clues to perhaps even more serious objective situations not overtly revealed. A single parent's frequent absences from work may indicate neither unreliability nor laziness, but may be due to a child's poor health or to anxiety about pressing debts. In either case, the underlying subjective factor, worry, is caused by an objective situation that may not be apparent at once to a personnel manager.

Knowledge of subjective factors may be necessary to make possible the formulation of objective plans with some probability that they will be carried out. A Travelers Aid worker returning runaway Mary to her family in another state knows that unless she talks to Mary long enough to find out her subjective attitude toward returning home, Mary may get off the bus at the next stop and foil the worker's plan for her safe return.

Moral Stereotyping

In addition to recognizing the difference between objective and subjective aspects of a situation, the interviewer should recognize the futility and even the danger involved in passing judgment on people's attitudes. Although a mile may seem short to you, to tell a woman who has walked that distance laboriously that she should not feel tired is useless, to say the least. To tell an emotionally upset person that he should be calm may succeed only in erecting a barrier against further expression of his difficulties.

The thermometer of a room may read seventy-two degrees, but the room may feel hot to some and cold to others. A statement about the temperature can be objectively verified or disproved, but to argue about the heat of the room is futile. Disagreement in such a case reflects only differences in subjective feelings, and insofar as one reports them sincerely, one is reporting correctly.

Although we can judge statements about objectively verifiable matters to be true or false, we are not similarly justified in passing judgments on subjective attitudes. Of two people waiting in line, one may sincerely feel the delay to be an imposition, and the other with equal sincerity may regard it as a matter of course. The requirements for eligibility for financial assistance in a public welfare agency may be objectively set, but to one client they may seem to involve an unwarranted intrusion into his personal affairs, whereas to another they may seem to represent only a wise, businesslike investigation. One applicant for a job may feel that the interviewer is prying into her private affairs; another, confronted by the same inquiries, may wonder why more information is not required. Not the passing of judgment as to the rightness or wrongness of such diverse attitudes, but the understanding of their causes, should be the aim of the interviewer, for only the latter will be helpful to him in dealing with the situation.

In another area, too, there is a natural but unjustified tendency to judge actions right or wrong. For example, divorce is absolutely taboo in some groups, whereas in others it is expected to occur with a certain normal frequency. The average American has long been converted to installment buying. But there are still some persons who believe that one should do without those things for which one does not have available cash. Each group tends to regard its own views as correct, the one condemning divorce or going into debt as wrong, the other holding that, in certain cases at least, it is completely justifiable. Social customs and laws change, and people alter their judgments of approval or condemnation.

It is essential for an interviewer to refrain from trying to impose his moral judgments on his clients. They should be allowed to discuss their feelings about pertinent matters without fear of condemnation. Knowledge of the flux of social attitudes on even basic ethical matters will tend to make an interviewer less absolute in his judgments of behavior. It would be desirable if he could refrain from making any such judgments about his clients, but since an interviewer, too, is human, he may find this godlike stance unattainable and discover that he does have strong feelings of condemnation toward some of their attitudes or behavior. The good interviewer will learn quickly, however, that any expression of such feelings blocks the progress of the interview. If his interest is genuinely centered in the client, he will learn to keep his personal feelings in the background.

Wisdom will warn the interviewer against hasty generalizations. He may tend not to trust in any matter a client who lies about his income and may regard as unreliable in other respects as well a youth who lies about his age in order to get a job. This all-or-none attitude permeates everyday thinking. People are regarded as all good or all bad, situations as completely right or thoroughly wrong. Such rigid classifications must be avoided by the interviewer who wishes to understand his client. He must recognize that there are shades and variations of rightness and wrongness. A person who lies about one subject may not lie about another. He may be so in need of a job that he will prevaricate no end to get one, but he may be scrupulously honest about financial matters. People who have fallen into "bad" modes of behavior in one area may be unusually "upright" in others.

"There is so much good in the worst of us, and so much bad in the best of us, that it ill behooves any one of us to find any fault with the rest of us." The truth of this saying is so clear that we can be sure that any judgment utterly condemning another person will be mistaken. The all-or-none principle fails. But, on the other hand, it is probably a mistake to try to assess accurately the precise respects in which a client is good and the precise ones in which he is bad. It is much more important to understand him and to seek the causes of his behavior, even when it is antisocial, than it is to grow indignant about it.

Conflicting Pulls

From birth on we have to make one choice after another. Some choices are relatively easy. In other situations we want to have our cake and eat it too. When forced to decide, we do so with much hesitation and often look back on our choice with some misgiving, wondering whether we have really chosen wisely. The student who gives up his fraternity beer party to study for an important examination feels the pull of the party very strongly while he tries to study. Sometimes the pull is so strong he reverses his choice and goes to the party, only then to feel the "voice of conscience" striving to pull him back to his work.

In many instances we resolutely put the thought of what we have rejected out of our mind—that is, our conscious mind. Nevertheless, the pull of what we have denied ourselves remains and sometimes takes its revenge in devious ways. When a choice has been difficult, we cannot deny the attractiveness of what we rejected merely by saying we do not want it. We do want it. What is true is only that under the circumstances we want it less than that which we have chosen. We want to lie abed in the morning, but we want to keep our jobs more. We want to keep slender, but we also want to nibble sweets. No matter which desire finally has its way with us, the defeated one is likely to rebel now and again.

Although some of us make up our minds more easily than others, we all experience many conflicting interests, desires, and emotions. The harboring of such conflicting feelings is technically known as ambivalence. An understanding of this concept is essential to anyone who is attempting to work successfully with people.

Sometimes an early conflict that was hard to resolve leaves us ambivalent about our choice long after the influences that led us to want what we rejected have ceased to exist. In such cases our ambivalence is not only unconscious but irrational as well. Nevertheless, it exists and has its adequate causes and effects. Anyone who would understand our behavior today will do so more adequately if he at least knows in general of the existence of unconscious and irrational ambivalence, even though he may not know the details of our own situation.

One common manifestation of ambivalence occurs in the areas of dependence and independence. Children want to grow up and have the privileges of adults—to spend their money as they like, to stay up late, and so on. At the same time they want to remain children—to play all day and to be free from responsibilities. This wish often carries into adulthood, so that even with chronological maturity many infantile desires continue to operate. Childhood food fads persist unchecked by adult knowledge. A man may marry primarily (although perhaps unconsciously) for mothering. It is only when the satisfactions of fulfilling adult responsibilities and obtaining adult privileges outweigh the desire for childhood pleasures that the individual grows up emotionally. All of us need to be loved, but for some of us this need causes conflict. We fear that accepting love will entail losing some of our cherished independence.

Superficial signs of dependence and independence are sometimes misleading. Here again we need to distinguish between objective and subjective aspects. A woman may be self-sufficient, an executive, and still subjectively be weighed down by a longing for dependence, thus using up a great deal of emotional energy day after day in her efforts to maintain herself in her own eyes as an independent adult.

Instances of ambivalence arise continually in interviewing. They are manifested by clients who clearly want help but are unable to ask for it, who ask advice but do not utilize it, who agree to certain plans but do not carry them out, who say one thing but by their behavior indicate the opposite.

The Relationship Between Interviewer and Interviewee

Parents are often amused at the enthusiasm their young son shows for his schoolteacher. He reports her comments on the weather, imitates her mannerisms, wants to take her gifts, is delighted if she asks him to clean the blackboard for her after school, and so on. Another parent whose child has the same teacher may not understand why she seems negativistic toward all the teacher's suggestions and seems to go out of her way to annoy and irritate the teacher. Similarly, adults themselves, when they stop to think about it, find that their strong attachments to or antagonisms for certain people seem unjustified by any conscious knowledge they have of the other's nature. Such positive and negative feelings toward those we come in contact with are universal phenomena, always present to some degree. Certain features of interviewing tend to intensify them, and for this reason the wise interviewer will want to understand their nature and effects and will seek to subject them to some measure of conscious control.

For many a client, talking with someone who listens with non-judgmental understanding instead of criticizing or admonishing is a unique experience. This relationship with a person who does not ask anything for himself personally, but focuses his interest entirely on the client and yet refrains from imposing advice or control, is a very satisfying one. The discovery of these characteristics in the interviewer, accompanied as it is by the absence of closer knowledge of the interviewer's personality with its inevitable personal whims and foibles, leads the client to idealize him. The client's feelings are unchecked by personal knowledge of the interviewer that might dilute them. Thus, he endows the worker with the ideal characteristics one is always searching for, quite independently of whether the worker actually is such an ideal person.

These feelings are usually not consciously revealed, but indications of them may be recognized in such comments from clients as: "It's been such a help to talk with you," "I see you understand," "You're the first person I've ever told this to," "What do you think I should do?" Remarks of this sort occur frequently in interviews.

The opposite sort of situation also arises in interviewing. Again, quite independently of the interviewer's actual character, the client, because of his own anxieties, insecurity, and deprivations, may endow him with negative characteristics and build up antagonism toward him. Much depends on the client's previous experiences with his parents or with others in authority. Negative feelings are often even more concealed than positive ones because of social standards of politeness, but they are revealed sometimes by the refusal to talk, by the breaking of an appointment, by refusal to return to the agency, or by trapping the worker into giving advice that can later be proved wrong.

The development of excessive negative or positive feelings by the client is often alarming to the interviewer who is unaware of having done anything to arouse such feelings. An interviewer wants his clients to like him, but sometimes in his eagerness to achieve this end he unwittingly encourages more dependency than he had realized was potentially present. A worker should realize that the development of an emotional rapport, positive or negative, between the client and himself is not abnormal but inevitable. He should direct his attention not to eliminating this relationship but to controlling its nature and intensity. He must guard against misleading the client into an overly dependent relationship by appearing too friendly or promising too much. However, he must not lean over backward in avoiding this danger and make the client feel that he is an unresponsive and unsympathetic listener. It is easy, when one is treated like a god, to assume a superior stance.

If an interviewer notices that the relationship with his client seems to be developing negatively, he should not become overly alarmed, because the client's attitude may be due not at all to the interviewer but to factors deeply hidden in his client's personality. He should review his own activity in interviews and make sure that he has given no objective grounds for the antagonism the client seems to feel toward him. He may have given inadequate help, broken an appointment, or have developed negative feelings toward the client of which he was not fully aware. If there are no such objective sources for his client's negativism, he can assure the client, by a continued attempt to understand the reasons for his difficulties, that he is not retaliating with disapproval of his own.

The development of an interrelationship of this general sort, positive or negative, between interviewer and interviewee is not at all a unique phenomenon but a universal one. It is essential that an interviewer recognize its existence in order to respond appropriately.

3 The interviewer's attitude

The importance of the interviewee's attitudes will have become clear by now. It is impossible to discuss the interviewee's attitudes and the conduct of an interview without commenting on the interviewer's attitudes at every point. All the things said about understanding human beings apply also to the interviewer, for he, too, is a human being, with unconscious as well as conscious motivation, ambivalence, prejudices, and objective and subjective reasons for his behavior. He brings to his relationship with the interviewee his own predetermined attitudes, which may profoundly affect that relationship. He has a natural tendency to impute to others personal feelings and may thus seriously misunderstand his client's situation and problem. If he is unable to bear frustration or poverty, he may find it difficult to comprehend his client's toleration of it. An interviewer who finds it difficult to reveal himself to others may decide that a client should not be "probed," when as a matter of fact the client wants nothing so much as to be helped to talk. We now discuss two of the many specific respects in which the interviewer needs to be particularly aware of his own feelings in order to be able to help the client satisfactorily.

Prejudices

Most of us often remark the prejudices of others but seldom are conscious of our own, for in our own case we regard them as natural opinions. When we are irritated or enthusiastic, when we react with anger, disgust, shame, pride, or love, it seems as if such situations would naturally cause such feelings in any normal person. A helpful step in discovering our own prejudices is to jot down a list of those we know others to possess. A little self-scrutiny will then convince us that these are not as alien to our attitudes as we may have assumed.

We usually think of prejudices as large, overall attitudes, such as race prejudice, class prejudice, religious prejudice, and political prejudice. Here we are concerned rather with much smaller matters, subtler and more easily escaping notice. We find exaggerated dislikes of sloppy dressers, flashy dressers, skinny people, fat people, show-offs, weak men, aggressive women, blondes, brunettes, or redheads. Elsewhere we find exaggerated fondness for blondes, brunettes, or redheads, pipe smokers, women with slender ankles, or men with curly hair. Some interviewers prefer rather self-sufficient clients who state their cases incisively; others prefer meek clients who need considerable help to express their needs; few can avoid responding with warm satisfaction to "grateful" clients.

A comparison of our list of prejudices with those of others will reveal the great variety in different individuals' attitudes toward the same sort of occurrence. For example, everyone has distinct ideas of his own as to what is really intolerable. Some can easily tolerate and attempt to understand the alcoholic but find a lazy person intolerable. For another laziness stirs no personal emotion but lying is an unpardonable sin: "I don't care what a person does so long as he is honest. I cannot bear to be deceived." Again, for others, even the most involved deception is passed over as a "white lie," but poor housekeeping is beyond the pale. A few find murder more easily acceptable than procrastination. Insofar as an interviewer can discover his areas of intolerance, his list of unpardonable sins, he has made a start toward self-disciplined control of his feelings in his relationships with others.

When an interviewer first learns that he should be nonjudgmental, should not become angry, should not become dependent upon the interviewee's affection and response, he tries to suppress his feelings, and as a result he tends to become artificial and stilted in his responses. It would be better to recognize the existence of such feelings and to learn to control their expression, because these feelings are not unnatural but merely inappropriate in the professional situation. If an interviewer is aware that he is becoming angry, he is then in a position to regulate his own feelings better than if he denies to himself that he has such feelings. Control of feelings, rather than absence of feelings, on the part of the worker is the goal.

Acceptance

We have spoken of the value of tolerance in an interviewer. But it is not easy to say how an interviewer can accept aberrant behavior or attitudes on the part of a client and yet maintain his own and the community's standards. Interviewers sometimes learn that they should be accepting without knowing very clearly what is involved in acceptance. Knowing the word gives them a false assurance that they understand its signficance.

In the training of the individual, certain standards of behavior are inevitably imposed, first by parents and later by society. It is natural that the individual, in learning to condemn his unacceptable behavior, should include in his condemnation similar behavior on the part of others. If, for example, he has learned to be neat, he tends to abhor slovenliness in others. The interviewer must learn to counteract this perfectly natural tendency to condemn all behavior that conflicts with his own standards. Toward almost every problem that a client brings, the interviewer has developed an attitude of approval or disapproval based on his own experiences, and he tends to assume that this attitude represents the norm. As his professional training and exprcrience grow, he recognizes that there is a wide range of individual variation in human responses to a given situation. This recognition may lead him to try to accept all such behavior, to refrain from evaluating it carefully. But this reaction clearly reveals an extremely limited understanding of the concept of acceptance, involving as it does only an arid, nonjudgmental impartiality. Real acceptance is primarily acceptance of the feelings given expression by behavior and does not necessarily involve acceptance of unsocial behavior at all; real acceptance involves positive and active understanding of these feelings and not merely passive refusal to pass judgment.

A passive attitude, of not passing judgment on a client's unusual behavior, is often interpreted by the client as approval of that behavior, a repudiation of a standard he himself accepts but has failed to live up to. He tends then either to reject the interviewer as an unfit guide or, at the other extreme, to continue and increase his undesirable behavior, thus trying out the interviewer to see how far he can go in his nonconformity. A man who makes no effort to get a job, for instance, may find his dilatoriness so accepted by the interviewer that he gradually gives up the struggle for self-maintenance entirely. A child whose petty stealing is ignored is not at all reassured, as she would be if she were confronted by the interviewer with knowledge of this misbehavior and yet convinced that in spite of what she has done the worker accepted her in the fuller sense of understanding her feelings and the emotional conflicts that induced her stealing. A child feels that a person who thus understands her is her friend. Such a person's recognition of her behavior will be regarded as a sign that he wants to help her overcome it.

To accept, then, is not to condone antisocial behavior, but to understand it in the sense of understanding the feelings it expresses. In a worker's early acquaintance with a client it is, of course, impossible to know, let alone understand specifically, all the various factors responsible for a given behavior. In such early stages we make use of the best knowledge we have available at that time, namely, the general familiarity we have acquired through theory and experience with the basic underlying dynamics of human behavior. We know that a person who appears angry and belligerent may, in fact, be feeling anxious and fearful. A person who appears demanding may have no other way to express his hurt pride and guilt about asking for advice or aid. Understanding of this sort lays the groundwork for real acceptance. As an interviewer's knowledge of the client deepens, however, his general knowledge is enlarged by an understanding of the particular pressures active in this specific situation. His general acceptance develops into more specific understanding. Such detailed understanding is not always possible, but the more definite it is, the more effective the worker can be.

Sometimes an interviewer, relying on his general understanding, says too readily, "I understand," and thus confuses and blocks the client in his attempt to present the details that would be needed for more specific understanding. The interviewer means that he wants to understand, or does understand in general, whereas the client realizes that he certainly does not yet know about the specific factors of his case. It often would be far better for the interviewer to say, "I do not understand"; then the client would realize that the interviewer wants to understand but needs more information.

Another easy error is to offer false reassurances. "I'm sure you'll soon be well." "I know you'll get a job soon." "Everything will be all right." Such remarks, far from reassuring the client, usually cause him to doubt the worker's understanding of the situation and consequently his ability to help. It would be more judicious and also more helpful to be realistic about the situation, to offer hope only when there are good grounds for it. The interviewer's recognition of the client's own doubts can itself be reassuring, for the client feels that he has in the interviewer someone who knows the worst and yet will still help him.

In the relationship between interviewer and interviewee, intellectual understanding is clearly insufficient unless it is accompanied by emotional understanding as well. Intellectual knowledge may suffice for mathematics or logic, but to understand intellectually the successive movements of dancing or skiing does not qualify one as a good dancer or skier. Similarly, in our relationships with other human beings, intellectual understanding is barren unless accompanied by emotional understanding. To know about emotions and feelings is not enough. One should be able to sense their existence and their degree and quality. Such ability does not come merely from reading a book such as this one or from classroom study, but requires the constant application of theoretical knowledge in practical day-to-day contact with human beings and their objective or subjective problems.

4 Purposes of interviewing

The method of conducting an interview will be influenced to a considerable extent by the purpose of the interview. As we have already noted, some interviews are directed primarily toward obtaining information, some primarily toward giving help; most, however, involve a combination of the two. The aim is to obtain knowledge of the problem to be solved and sufficient understanding of the person troubled and of the situation so that the problem can be solved effectively. Whether these two functions of understanding and helping are combined in one agency or interviewer or divided among several will modify the details of the methods used but not their essentials.

One early caution is worth noting. The interviewer is sometimes so anxious to help that he rushes ahead without first obtaining a sound understanding of the situation. That such a procedure can be destructive rather than helpful should be clear. To advise a young man to continue in college without first obtaining knowledge of his interest and abilities is clearly unwise. The first and basic purpose of interviewing is to obtain understanding of the problem, of the situation, and of the client who has come for help.

Another caution to be kept in mind throughout is that although the interviewer should be clearly aware of his purposes, it is not always wise to seek to realize them by direct action. Even when considerable information is desired, it is often best obtained by encouraging the client to talk freely of his problem rather than by asking such a pointed question as "Were you fired from your last job?" People are sensitive about their personal lives, family skeletons, poverty, past mistakes, and so on, and early flat-footed inquiry may only alienate a client and cause him to erect protective barriers against what may well seem to him unwarranted intrusion. Once convinced of the worker's sensitive understanding, of his desire to know not out of wanton curiosity but only in order to help, and of the confidential nature of the relationship, the client will welcome an opportunity to talk about things that earlier he would have suppressed.

The specific kind of help an interviewer can give, and consequently the specific sort of information he will seek, are determined to a considerable extent by the functions of his agency. He may, for example, want to obtain the kind of information that will be needed to give medical aid, or the kind needed for financial assistance, child placement, or employment. Within this general field he will be guided by the indications his client gives him of the special facts involved in this particular case. He will first listen to his client's statement of his needs and then guide the interview along those channels that seem most appropriate to the specific circumstances of the situation. A good general alters his strategy for reaching a given objective according to changes in the situation, and a good interviewer will modify his techniques as circumstances demand.

The information to be sought by an interviewer is sometimes fixed in advance by a printed form or specific instructions from the interviewer's superior. In such cases it is essential that the interviewer be thoroughly acquainted with the purposes back of each question and understand its significance. Otherwise he tends to ask the questions in a perfunctory manner that minimizes their importance to the interviewee and raises doubts as to the significance of the interview. Further, an interviewer is inclined to accept superficial and inadequate answers to questions whose purport he has not grasped. Unless he understands the purpose of obtaining certain information or carrying out certain plans for the client, he will frequently be unable to do either effectively.

For example, an interviewer asked simply to obtain a developmental history of a highly distressed man who has suddenly left his job may do so in a perfunctory manner that will miss many significant details. If, however, he knows some of the ways in which a psychiatrist may use such information in helping a man who has had a sudden breakdown, he will be able to do a more adequate job.

The interviewee, too, should be helped to feel that each question is important and significant. In addition to the presence of this conviction on the part of the interviewer, it may be necessary to explain, in a way that will satisfy the interviewee, the relevance of the questions to his own needs and interests. A question as to one's birthplace may seem irrelevant until one realizes its importance in determining citizenship. A question as to what floor the client lives on assumes more significance if he is afflicted with a heart ailment; questions about diet are called for when a person has high blood pressure; early developmental history has special significance in children's behavior problems; the number of jobs held in the past ten years is important in gauging a client's employability.

Every interview has, to begin with, its manifest purpose. If an agency has initiated an interview and called someone in, the person interviewed can usually be put most quickly at his ease—relieved of uncertainty in the face of the unknown—and the interview most quickly advanced by a straightforward statement, in terms the client can readily grasp, of the interviewer's purpose in asking him to come in for a consultation. When the interviewee asks for the appointment, the situation is a little different. In such cases, rather than greet the client with a barrage of questions, it is better to let him state in his own words his problem and his purpose in coming in for an interview. Sometimes the client is nervous and incoherent, but he is most quickly reassured if he is allowed to begin the interview in his own way. Often the interviewer can learn much from the very hesitancy and indirect way in which the client approaches the account of his difficulty.

The worker will, of course, keep in mind the specific functions of his agency, because these may delimit rather sharply the area in which he can be of service. Sometimes he can help most by referring the client to some other agency whose ability to aid will be more pertinent to his needs. Ordinarily, however, even a referral should not be made immediately, for often the manifest purpose of the client differs considerably from his real purpose, and the latter may well fall within the field of the given agency or require referral to a quite different agency from the one that first comes to the interviewer's mind. A woman, with three children, applying for a job may need first of all an opportunity to clarify her own thoughts as to whether she wants to work and place her children in a day care center or whether she wants to seek financial assistance from a public welfare agency in order to stay at home. Only after this question has been settled can we know where to refer her.

Most people who come seeking help or advice are considerably troubled by their problems, as is evidenced by the fact that their anxieties have risen to such a pitch as to drive them to take the step of seeking this consultation. This anxiety may make it difficult for them to see their problems distinctly or state them clearly. Very often their problems will be so involved that they are unable to come anywhere near locating the root of the trouble. A man who comes in to register for a job may really need medical attention. A woman who expresses anxiety about the development of her children may have more real need to discuss her troubled relationship with her husband.

The inexperienced interviewer should keep in mind the possibility that his client is suffering from some trouble more difficult than he realizes or is able to state. He will endeavor by various methods to put his client at ease, to stimulate him to talk relatively freely about his problem, and to help him to organize his own confused thoughts and feelings about his difficulties. Sometimes talking about the situation to a sympathetic listener will itself lead to a satisfactory conclusion. The client's thoughts may thus be organized so clearly that he himself sees what action he should take. His fears and hesitancies may be removed, and he may be encouraged to take whatever action is necessary. More often, perhaps, just talking is not enough, and help of other sorts will be required. We shall discuss some of these subjects later. Our purpose now is to call attention to the desirability of looking beyond manifest purposes to more fundamental latent ones that may be present.

It is, of course, possible to probe too far. Some sleeping dogs should be left undisturbed, particularly when the interviewer is not equipped to deal with them should they be aroused. Even a skilled interviewer should use a good deal of discretion and wisdom in going beneath the surface.

The fact that interviews bring to light new knowledge of purposes and needs as well as new information about the relevant facts implies that the interviewer should not let his plan of action be unalterably fixed in advance or determined early in the interview. A certain amount of flexibility is always desirable.

5 How to interview

Although the most skillful interviewing gives the appearance of being a smooth and spontaneous interchange between the interviewer and the interviewee, the skill thus revealed is obtained only through careful study and years of practice. For purposes of study it is possible to break down an interview into a number of component parts and discuss each separately. In actual interviewing, of course, no such sharp breaks occur. The interviewer must become conscious of the various subtleties in interviewing before he can absorb them into his spontaneous responses. First recognized in theory, they later become so much a part of the worker's skill that they are utilized naturally at each step without conscious notice. We hear much of the intuitive skill of the trained interviewer. But back of such skill lies much study of the various processes and interrelationships involved in interviewing. The skillful skier is unconscious of the many movements integrated in his smooth flight, but earlier he had to learn them painfully, one by one, and then learn to combine them into a harmonious, coordinated whole.

One danger that arises from an analytical treatment such as we must necessarily undertake is that an interviewer, in his attempt to find a few simple rules that will guide him, will seize certain techniques that are highly valuable in certain situations and apply them in others in which they are less relevant. Supervisors notice that the words of a caseworker reported in a case and discussed favorably in a staff meeting begin to recur time and again in the reports of their students. Each technique suggested has its limitations and should be used only on appropriate occasions and in conjunction with other techniques that are equally demanded by the whole situation. In practice none of the methods to be discussed operates in a vacuum, but only in relation with most of the others.

Observation

In one sense all that we shall say about interviewing might well come under the heading of observation. Here we shall discuss a few of the simpler and more obvious types of observation important in all interviewing. It goes almost without saying that we should observe what the interviewee says. It is less obvious that we should note equally what he does not say, what significant gaps there are in his story. We should note also such things as bodily tensions, flushing, excitability, and dejection because they supplement, and sometimes even belie, the picture given by the client's words. The following opening sentences of the report of an interview reveal how much is told by the physical behavior of the client.

Mrs. Marsh came to the office asking for temporary financial assistance. I noticed her sitting in the waiting room before my interview with her. She was sitting erectly, almost rigidly, and was clenching her hands in her lap. Her face was white and drawn. When she came into my office, she was so tense and nervous that she could hardly speak. She sat on the edge of her chair, looking directly at me and wringing her hands. A large, well-built woman with blonde hair, extremely blue eyes, and light skin, she appeared to have a severe case of acne, which marred her complexion. When I asked Mrs. Marsh to tell me how I might help her, she spoke in short, jerky sentences and told her story in no logical sequence.

Out of all the things to be observed, each interviewer will remark only a relatively small number. His selection wil be determined by his own observational equipment as limited by his interests, prejudices, attitudes, and training. Because it seems impossible to take note of things without adding a personal element of interpretation, he may even modify considerably in his own picture of the situation the data actually presented to him. To illustrate this influence of the observer's own nature on his reports, the following experiment is sometimes conducted in an early session of a casework class.

Students are asked to write, in no more than a page, an observation they have made of an individual or a group of individuals. The observation may take place in a restaurant, at a bus station, on the street, or on the campus. Students are asked to perform this experiment in pairs; two students observe the same scene and write it up without comparing notes. These parallel papers are then read in class. Such a project is unusually convincing in illustrating the subjective variations of the observer. Sometimes the reports are so different that the students cannot believe they are of the same situation. In one an individual is described as angry, callous to the pleas of his child for an ice-cream cone. In the other he is reported as anxious, uncertain, indecisive, frustrated, and helpless in the face of a demanding offspring in a temper tantrum. A project of this sort directs a student's attention to the limitations of his own capacity to see what is actually happening and to his tendency to distort the objective facts with his own preconceived ideas of what he himself would feel or do in such a situation.

That we cannot take for granted that our observation of an individual is accurate is initially a blow to our self-confidence. It is a blow, however, that may help to break down any preconceived ideas about our infallibility and pave the way to self-scrutiny and the development of a more observant capacity to size up situations as they really are. It comes at first as a surprise that what seems like anger to one person may be sensed as anxiety by another. What seems like cocky self-assurance to one may be sensed as tense insecurity by another. What seems like "sweetness and light" to one may be recognized as hostility by another. Such differences in interpretation arise partly from the facts that people do not always behave and act as they feel, that they do not always say what they really mean, and that they do not always behave logically and rationally. But in part, the differences are due to the fact that everyone looks at the rest of the world from his own immediate point of view, which always seems to him the natural, logical, sensible one. When an interviewer realizes that a client's point of reference seems like the reasonable one to him, it becomes clear that it is important to attempt to understand how the situation looks from his viewpoint and why that seems to him to be the only correct way of looking at things. If we attempt to see the client's point of view before trying to persuade him to accept what seems to us a more logical point of view, we may have a faint beginning of understanding him.

Many times a client finds the interviewer the first person in his experience who can listen understandingly and yet not intrude upon his feelings or attempt to redirect his behavior. This experience for the client is sometimes surprisingly satisfying. As just noted, it alone is sometimes helpful. At other times it is merely one part of a helping process.

That people do not always say what they mean or act as they

feel is continually apparent in interviewing. For example, case-workers in public welfare agencies repeatedly have the experience of having a client storm into the office belligerently demanding immediate financial support, only to have him reveal, when met with kindness, that he is really frightened, ashamed of his poverty, and pleading for understanding of the trouble in which he finds himself.

Listening

One type of observation comes through listening, one of the fundamental operations of interviewing. It goes without saying that a good interviewer is a good listener, but what constitutes a good listener? One who frequently interrupts to say what he would have done under similar circumstances is not a good listener, but neither is he who sits quietly and says nothing. Absence of response may easily seem to the talker to reflect absence of interest. Everyone knows from his own experience in telling a story that people like a listener who indicates by relevant comments or questions that he has grasped the essential points of one's tale and who adds illuminating comments on certain significant features of one's account that have not been stressed and might well have been overlooked by an inattentive listener. This attention to important details that have not been emphasized gives the storyteller the stimulating feeling that the listener not only wants to, but does, understand to an unusual degree what he is trying to say.

A common error of an inexperienced interviewer is to be embarrassed by silences and to feel that he must fill them with questions or comments. A decent respect for silences is often more helpful. Sometimes the person interviewed falls silent because he is reluctant to go on with what comes next in his story or because he does not quite know how to formulate what he plans to say. A hasty interruption may leave this important part of the story forever unsaid. Sometimes, of course, a silence is due to other causes and, if allowed to continue, will only embarrass the person interviewed. In such cases, a pertinent remark or question will encourage him to continue.

Listening to a client's story is sometimes helpful in and of itself. Everyone knows the value at times of "letting off steam." When something happens that upsets a person or "makes him mad," he tends to get over these feelings more quickly if he can find a sympathetic friend who will let him "rave" for a while. Relieved, he can then go ahead and use his energy more constructively. Without this opportunity to talk it out with someone else, he may "boil" for days. He probably does not want anyone to tell him what to do or what he should have done differently but may merely want someone to listen and understand how upset he is. It is unfortunate that the average lay person is not a good listener. He usually feels impelled to point out the other person's mistakes and faults or to give advice.

The following report of an interview from an employment agency illustrates how valuable mere listening can be:

Mrs. Cobb came in to register for a job, but there was such difficulty with simple matters, such as name, address, and former jobs, and she seemed so upset that I said perhaps she felt these details were not important, and possibly we should talk about a definite job for her first. She said she did not mind very much about answering the questions, but she did not know what she would do if she should get a job. I asked how she meant this, and she said that everything at home was all upset and it kept her worried all the time. I replied that many people felt they could talk only about employment when they came to this agency, but we were interested in helping people in every way possible, and I knew there were many things besides a job that could be worrisome. She said that I had "certainly told the truth that time," and proceeded to tell a very long and involved story about many troubles with her husband, children, death in the family, and so on. When she had finished, I said that she certainly had had many troubles and I should like to help her if she felt there was something I could do. She said she thought she could manage everything by herself, but that day she had been walking all over town worrying to herself and was "nearly crazy" and felt she just had to talk to somebody. She said that she did not often get this way, but when she did she just had to talk to someone. After she talked she always felt better, but she felt best when she talked to somebody who knew "what it is all about." I said that we had used up a great deal of time and that there was someone else waiting to see me, but I should be glad to make an appointment for her to come back to talk either about the job or something else we might be able to do for her. In preparing to leave, she said she did not think it necessary to come back because she thought that things were going to be better and she had a part-time job that helped out with family expenses. She seemed much more cheerful than when she came in, and I remarked that I was glad we were able to help her even if all we gave her was conversation. She replied that I was still young and someday I would learn that "conversation is a wonderful thing."

There is, however, a danger in allowing the client undirected expression of his feelings. The feelings may be due not to a recent upsetting experience, but to a long chain of experiences going back into the remote past. These early experiences may have become twisted and distorted and interrelated with other things through the years, so that mere talking does not bring relief. The client's need to talk may not be occasional but constant, and if the interviewer encourages too much release of feeling, areas may be opened up with which both interviewer and client are unequipped to cope. In general, catharsis through talking is more effective when the disturbing feeling is related to a fairly recent experience, and it becomes of dubious value when the feeling is due to long-repressed experiences. If a difficult situation can be immediately aired, the danger of its being pushed from consciousness but remaining an active source of anxiety is lessened. If a person has had a hairbreadth automobile escape, he feels better if he can talk about it a lot for a while, for then its importance gradually wanes and is forgotten. It is helpful to remember, particularly with children, that if they do have a traumatic experience—an accident, an operation, a sexual assault—the more immediately they can be helped to express their feelings about it, the less will be the danger of its becoming a source of neurotic conflict. It is as if the wound should be kept open long enough to drain off the infection in order to avoid a festering sore.

Listening Before Talking or "Begin where the Client Is"

The first step in an interview is to help the interviewee relax and feel fairly comfortable. Naturally it is difficult to help the interviewee relax unless the interviewer himself is relaxed. Sometimes the client can quickly be put at ease by letting him state his purpose in coming, sometimes by giving him a brief account of why he was asked to come. In either case, an advisable next step is to encourage him to talk and then to listen carefully while he speaks of what is on the "top" of his mind in connection with the interview. Listening to the client gives the interviewer a chance to become acquainted with him, to know what language he speaks, literally and figuratively. It makes clear the kind of questions, comments, and suggestions that should later be directed to him and the way in which they should be formulated. It is as unsatisfactory to use literary language with a person used to the vernacular as it is to use slang expressions with a professor totally unfamiliar with them.

Even when our primary interest in a given interview is to obtain the answers to a set of questions, we can profit much from letting the client talk rather freely at first. He will usually reveal the answers to many questions without their being asked and often will suggest the best methods of approach for obtaining any additional information that is required.

When suggestions are to be made by the interviewer, it is even more important to let the client express himself first. Sometimes he will even suggest the course of action that the interviewer intends to advise. In this situation his suggestion can simply be confirmed and strengthened, and the fact that he regards it as coming from himself will make it more likely that he will carry it out. Other clients may reveal a deep-seated hostility to the suggestions about to be made. When this occurs, the interviewer is warned to proceed with caution and to attempt to discover and remove or modify the emotional causes of the hostility before proposing his plan.

Another advantage in letting the interviewee talk first is that it tends to counteract any preconceived ideas about him that the interviewer may have allowed himself to entertain. It gives the interviewer the advantage of being able to see the situation and the client's problem from the client's point of view. Because it is the client who eventually must act, it is clearly advantageous to start from where he is rather than from some vantage point of the interviewer, even though the latter might be superior.

If someone comes in and asks for a job and the interviewer proceeds at once to make a number of suggestions, he may well be surprised later to find that the client has adopted no one of them. Upon further examination the worker may then find out what he might well have discovered in the first interview if he had done more listening and less talking—that the client's real worry was that he could not hold a job if he got one, or that he did not see how he could take a job because his wife and children were sick at home and needed constant care.

Questioning

Perhaps the central method of interviewing is the fine art of questioning. We shall discuss only a few of its many features.

Abrupt or tricky questions are inappropriate in a casework interview. The method of the casework interview is the method of friendliness, the method of asking questions in order to understand and be of assistance. Clients soon recognize the attitudes of their interviewers and tend to respond to the best of their abilities when

they feel the presence of a real desire to understand and to help.

The interviewer who puts his questions accusingly or suspiciously arouses only fear and suspicion, not cooperation. The wording of the question is often of less importance than the manner and tone of voice in which it is put. The interviewer's safeguard here is really to be interested in understanding and aiding; then his manner and tone are very likely to reflect that interest. The question, "Are you looking for work?" may sound suspicious, accusing, sarcastic, or friendly, depending upon how it is expressed, and that expression in turn reflects how the interviewer really feels.

Interviewers who are just beginning to find out about the influence of unconscious desires and emotions on human behavior sometimes come to enjoy the discovery of some hidden motive or influence so much that they cannot resist letting the client know that they "see through" him. They experience the joy of the amateur detective and, by revealing this attitude, alienate their clients. The more mature understanding that comes with experience in helping others leads them instead to feel increased sympathy with a person in such distress that he had been forced to conceal important facts even from himself.

A similar error consists in becoming so interested in the mysterious realms of the unconscious that the interviewer probes his client unnecessarily to satisfy his interest in the esoteric. Although probing for a bullet is pretty painful, mental probing can be far worse, and realization of this fact should cause an interviewer to carry his inquiry only as far as is necessary for him to be helpful.

A good general rule is to question for only two purposes—to obtain specifically needed information and to direct the client's conversation from fruitless to fruitful channels. Examples of the latter would be questions that encourage him to talk in relevant areas in which he finds the going difficult and remarks such as "I don't quite understand," which will help him to elaborate more fully.

Most people tend to ask either too many questions or too few. Each interviewer should study his own tendency and seek to curb it. Too many questions will confuse and block the client, whereas too few may place too much of the burden of the interview on him and may leave salient areas unexplored.

In general, leading, rather than pointed, questions and questions that cannot be answered by a brief "yes" or "no" are preferred. They stimulate the client to talk freely and avoid the always present danger of putting answers into his mouth. Even if questions that imply an answer do not result in false answers, they tend to give the impression that the questioner is lacking in fundamental understanding of the situation. "Would five dollars be enough?" is not as good a query as "How much do you need?"

A questioner should, of course, try to adjust his pace to that of his client. To go too slowly suggests lack of interest or understanding. To push ahead too fast is to miss important clues, to confuse the client, and to suggest in a different way that we are not really interested in what he has to say. Again, we must accept the client's pace in the sense of not pushing him to reveal more than he is prepared to at any one time. To ask him to reveal confidences before we have won his confidence is to court defeat.

There are no magical questions that can be used on all occasions as the good fairy uses her wand. Sometimes in reading a case record, a student comes across a question that was so timely and effective that he is tempted to use it in his own next interviews and is surprised that it does not bring the same rewarding results. In general, we seem to get further by being encouraging and sympathetic, by leading the client to talk freely, than by trying to drag information out of him by belaboring him with questions.

Talking

Closely allied to questions are the comments of the interviewer. Sometimes the only difference between the two lies in the speaker's inflection. "You found your last job pretty difficult" is either a query or a comment, depending on whether one raises or lowers the pitch of the last syllables. In any case, both questions and comments are species of talking, and certain rules hold for both. In general, the interviewer should comment only for purposes similar to those for which he asks questions—to reassure or encourage the interviewee, to lead him on to discuss further relevant matters, and so on. The one additional kind of talking that goes beyond these purposes is the definite giving of information or advice. As suggested earlier, this stage should come after the interviewer is familiar enough with the client's situation to know whether suggestions will be acceptable or pertinent.

There is a great difference between expressing a meaning and communicating a meaning. Because the latter is the aim of the interviewer, he must devote considerable care to his manner of expression. He must "think with wisdom" but speak the language of his client, including as far as possible the idiom of the client.

So often words used by one group are not understood by another. This tendency not to be understood is especially true of technical words, such as resources, siblings, and eligibility, and of the specialized terms of such fields as law, medicine, and psychiatry. But also many everyday terms are used with quite different senses by different people. A person given to exaggeration may describe as "catastrophic" an event that another would call "a slight accident." The difficulty of transmitting meaning is aptly illustrated by questionnaires. How many who have filled out the pesky things have ever understood all the questions? An interviewer who remembers his perplexities on such occasions can readily sympathize with his clients and even anticipate some of their difficulties.

It is not enough that all the words used by the interviewer should be understood; it is important that they be understood as they were meant. For example, many caseworkers bandy about such terms as love, hate, anger, and hostility in a loose way, meaning to include weak emotions as well as strong ones, whereas to many a client anger involves at least such overt phenomena as flushing of the face, clenching of the fists, and rapid increase of heartbeat and respiration. The worker who tells his client, "I know you were angry with me for missing our last appointment," seems to the client to be grossly overstating the case.

Answering Personal Questions

Interviewers are frequently troubled by the personal questions clients ask them. Sometimes they are embarrassed and do not know what to answer or indeed whether to answer. If we can judge correctly the reasons back of such questions, the appropriate response will often be indicated.

A client may ask personal questions merely because he wants to be polite or thinks it is the social thing to do. He may not be interested in the answers, and in such cases if the discussion is directed back to his own problems, he will be glad to continue with what is to him a much more absorbing subject, himself.

Often, questions related to the worker's age, marital status, parenthood, or educational background may indicate simply the interviewee's natural curiosity about the person to whom he is telling so much.

Again, personal questions may indicate the beginning of the establishment of that closer relationship between the interviewer and the interviewee discussed in chapter two. The interviewee is interested in finding out something about the personality and interests of the interviewer. He is testing him out, wanting to know what sort of person he is in order to know whether his real personality corresponds to the one the interviewee is beginning to picture in his mind.

In most instances, a brief, truthful answer to a personal question is desirable. Normally the answer should be followed by an immediate redirection of the client's attention to himself. One danger is that the interviewer, through embarrassment, may become involved and tell too much, more than the client is really interested in knowing. This kind of response directs the client away from his own problems rather than toward them.

At other times, an interviewer becomes involved in personal questions because he has failed to grasp their significance. Often such queries are not really personal but constitute rather the client's way of introducing a problem of his own that he would like to have discussed.

An older adolescent boy absorbed with the problem of whether to marry may be trying to give the worker an indication of this concern and his desire to discuss it by a question, "Why aren't you married?" A brief impersonal answer leading to a question about his own ideas about marriage will open the way for the client to pursue his own problems, which may involve such things as worry over leaving his mother or fear he cannot support a wife.

Novice women interviewers occasionally find it difficult to maintain a professional relationship with a male client. In their eagerness to be helpful they sometimes overrespond and, without realizing it, lead the interviewee to believe that they are personally interested in him. Then they are very much embarrassed when asked for a date. They have failed to make clear in their manner the professional nature of the relationship. Had they done so, the interviewee, though attracted, would have gauged the interviewer's interest correctly as a friendly desire to help. The same misinterpretation of the relationship can occur, of course, with a male interviewer and female client.

When such misinterpretation of the professional nature of the relationship does occur, instead of becoming frightened and withdrawn, the interviewer can best handle the situation by frankly telling the client that she feels she can be of most help if she sees him only during interviews and if they direct their discussion primarily to his difficulties. At the same time she should scrutinize her own attitude to make certain that she has not fallen into certain mannerisms that would lead a client to expect too much from her.

Sometimes an interviewer deliberately introduces his own personal interests into the discussion. He may admire the interviewee's flower or dog and add comments about his own likes and dislikes.

Or, to encourage the client to talk about his early experience, he may tell the client that he, too, is from Texas and reminisce with him about the locality and people mutually known, or he may even enter into a discussion of politics, unions, or religion. Although at times such devices may be successful in helping the interviewee to feel acquainted and relaxed, the value of their use, except in rare instances, is dubious. Their dangers outweigh their possible value. With the introduction of the interviewer's personal opinions and feelings, the relationship may leave the professional level and become a social give-and-take or, worse, an argument. It is better for the interview to proceed with the client as the focus of attention, for his ideas and opinions, rather than the interviewer's, are paramount in the professional relationship.

Interviewers sometimes make the error of trying to win the client's approval by commenting on the attractiveness of his clothes or the appearance of his home. There is a distinction between an honest, natural appreciation of such things and flattery or patronage. If the interviewer's interest is genuine, an expression of it may help in furthering the interview, but if it is a technique whose purpose is to flatter the client, this artificial intrusion will be sensed by the client. A saccharine effusiveness on the part of the interviewer is as offensive to a troubled person as irritability.

Leadership or Direction

From all that has been said thus far it may seem as if the interviewer assumes very little activity and direction, because so much stress has been put upon leaving the client free to express himself in his own way. Indeed, the inexperienced interviewer often feels as if the client were running away with the situation—setting the topics for discussion and determining the pace of the conversation—so that all the poor interviewer can do is to keep track of what is being said. Actually, however, the skilled interviewer does assume leadership throughout. He consciously decides to allow the client to express himself. He knows the function and policy of his agency. He knows, in general, the areas in which he may be of service to the client. With these things in mind, he guides the conversation along paths that enable him to determine whether he is going to be able to help the client and, if so, in what respects.

He first directs his questions along the lines of allowing the interviewee to express his need in sufficient detail so that he may understand him better and know whether he will be able to help or whether he will need later to refer the client to someone else. He unobtrusively directs the interview throughout, deciding when to listen, when to talk, what to observe, and so on. With the overtalkative person who is inclined to ramble, or the person whose mind tends to wander, he gently and sympathetically leads the interviewee back and redirects him through leading questions to a discussion of the immediate situation.

The difficulty in acquiring the appropriate degree of leadership in interviewing is well illustrated by the following report from a beginning student of casework:

At first I seemed to be off somewhere when opportunities presented themselves to guide the client in expressing his feeling at a given moment. I sat like a stick, and when later asked by my supervisor why I had not done this or said that, I answered, "I don't know." Then I went to the opposite extreme. I progressed not only to the point where I learned to insert "Why?" but I carried questioning so far that often, as was pointed out to me later, I had switched what was on the client's mind to some other track. However, I am learning to listen again. It's a different sort of listening than I did when I sat petrified lest by speaking I stop the client's flow of conversation entirely. It is a more intelligent listening that is the outgrowth of the little bit more assurance I have. I am beginning to listen because I realize it is what my client wants, rather than because I do not know what to say that may help him express himself. If I do ask a question or say something, it is to show him I understand or want to help him say what he is finding it difficult to tell me and not, as previously, because I am shaky in my position and feel I have to say something so he'll know I am there and that I am the interviewer. You learn and learn, and what remains to be learned seems to grow and grow.

The question of what material is relevant is not so simple as it might seem. Frequently, material that seems irrelevant to the inexperienced has, because of the common tendency to disguise and distort and misplace one's feelings, considerable significance. It may be necessary to let the client ramble on for a while in order to clear the decks, as it were, so that he can get down to things that really are on his mind. On the other hand, with an already disturbed person it may be important for the interviewer to know when to discourage further elaboration of upsetting material, especially if the worker would be unable to do anything about it. An inexperienced interviewer might, for instance, be intrigued with the bizarre elaboration of material that the psychotic produces, but further elaboration of this material might encourage the client in his instability. A too random discussion may indicate that the interviewee is not certain of the areas in which the interviewer is prepared to help him, and he may be seeking some direction. Or again, satisfying though it may be for the interviewer to have the interviewee tell him intimate details, such revelations sometimes need to be checked, or encouraged only in small doses. An interviewee who has "talked too much" often reveals subsequent anxiety. Such a reaction is illustrated by the fact that after a "confessional" interview the interviewee frequently surprises the interviewer by being withdrawn, inarticulate, or hostile or by breaking the next appointment.

In certain types of interviewing the interviewer is called upon to give advice and to offer suggestions, sometimes to formulate concrete plans of action and even to bring some influence to bear on the client to adopt a plan of procedure. It is always a problem how far direction of this sort should be carried.

The interviewer in a social agency is there primarily to serve the client. His problem is how best to make his help effective. Many of his clients come seeking advice. They feel that a person in the interviewer's position is equipped to give expert advice, and they expect that when they ask for it, it will be proffered them. If the interviewer has sound advice to give and if his client is free enough of conflict to be able to accept it, it is probably wise to offer it. In many instances, however, advice is futile because the client is unable to act upon it. A woman in emotional conflict over her husband finds it difficult to accept advice either to divorce him or to remain with him. We can point out in such cases the probable consequences of the various alternatives that are available and stimulate the client to a course of reflection that may enable her to reach a decision for herself. For example, we can make clear the possibilities of getting a job, the legal procedures that would be necessary for a divorce, the steps to be taken in getting public assistance, the possibilities of aiding her husband to make a better home adjustment, and so on.

Frequently, people who ask for advice really do not need it. Usually they have had plenty of that from relatives, neighbors, the clergy, or doctors. What they need is assistance in freeing themselves from some of the confusions in which they have become bogged down—additional information that will throw light on their situation and encouragement to come to a decision of their own.

There are times when it is helpful to give a bit of advice to the client who demands it in order to test out his ability to use it, to challenge the mobilization of his energies so that both he and the interviewer may see more clearly whether he is able to profit from suggestions. Again, a bit of harmless advice may merely be a symbol to the client of our interest in him and willingness to try to help, whereas our rigid refusal to make suggestions may seem to the client an unwillingness to help.

Frequently the client who asks, "What do you think I should do?"—even the client who comes in with an eviction notice and seems to dump it helplessly in the interviewer's lap—when questioned as to whether he has any plans actually has several resourceful ideas. If a worker who is asked for advice gives it because, perhaps, he fears that if he did not his prestige with the client would be threatened, he is really failing to utilize the client's own resourcefulness. In a surprising number of instances, the client who in turn is asked, "What do you think?" comes forward with ideas and plans of his own.

It is still more difficult to know when, if ever, an interviewer should go so far as to try to persuade a client to a course of action that he is reluctant to adopt but that seems to the worker clearly indicated. "A man convinced against his will is of the same opinion still." Many a persuasive interviewer has been disappointed by subsequent events. A battered wife who is persuaded to take legal action to have her husband prevented from assaulting her blames the interviewer if her husband subsequently leaves town and she is forced to apply for public assistance. Yet it would be as much a mistake not to inform her of the legal recourse available and let her make a choice among the alternatives. There is a distinction between persuading people against their will and offering them a possible plan of action.

The casework interviewer should remember that his primary aim is to help his clients. If this desire is his basic driving one, he need not be overly fearful that he will appear too inquisitive or too authoritative. There are occasions, especially in certain types of cases, when an interviewer represents some degree of authority to the client. If, however, his feelings are centered on the welfare of his client, this fact will break through the barrier of his authoritative position and be recognized by the client. If, on the other hand, the interviewer is absorbed in his own fears that the client will not like him and hence will not talk, or will regard him as prying, then indeed the client will sense the interviewer's uncertainty and come to distrust his motives.

When possible, it is desirable not to appear to exercise authority, but to lead the client to take whatever steps are necessary for himself. In general, the things people do for themselves have more meaning for them.

If people find their own jobs, look for their own housing, make their own applications to hospitals or other agencies, they are more likely to carry plans through. One person's way may not always be the same as another's, but each person has to work out his own manner of meeting situations. We must allow people a large measure of self-determination.

On the other hand, a worker should not allow his theory of self-determination to become a cloak behind which he withholds giving the client the help really needed. It is possible to give so little direction that the client profits not at all and is not even helped to know what kind of assistance is available.

Interpretation

The interviewer's first aim, as we have said repeatedly, is to understand as fully as possible his client's problem. To achieve this understanding, he must interpret the many clues to the underlying situation that the client presents through his behavior and conversation. Rarely is the client sufficiently conscious of his own self to know and be able to give a straightforward account of the crucial factors that lie at the base of his difficulty. The interviewer must discover these factors himself by going beneath the surface of his client's remarks and understanding their more than superficial significance. Just as a physician must look beyond the symptoms, say, fever or a bad cough, to the cause of his patient's illness, say, pneumonia or tuberculosis, so the casework interviewer must look for the underlying anxiety or fear that is symptomatically indicated by hostility or dependency or chronic invalidism.

Juvenile stealing, for example, may express merely a desire to be "one of the gang," or an unrealized need for revenge because of harsh home discipline, or, of course, any one of many other things. Failure in reading on the part of a child with a high I.Q. may be due to poor eyesight but is more likely to be a consequence of some emotional conflict, such as ambivalence about growing up or fear of competition with a younger sibling.

The experienced interviewer will constantly be framing hypotheses as to the basic factors in the case confronting him, testing these, rejecting most of them, tentatively retaining others, seeking further confirmation, and so on. For example, when a woman in speaking of her husband "accidentally" refers to him as her father, the alert interviewer notes this reference but does not jump to the conclusion that her relationship to her husband is to an unusual degree that of daughter to father. He recognizes the idea as one possibility and keeps his attention open for corroborating evidence. In practice many of the tentative hypotheses one forms have to be discarded. Flexibility, the ability to change our hypothesis with the appearance of new evidence, is a trait well worth cultivating.

For an interviewer to interpret for himself is essential; for him to pass his interpretations on to the client is usually inadvisable. It is tempting to reveal our discoveries, for example, to say to a client, "Your blustering shows that you are really afraid." But if an interviewer is interested in helping the client, he will ordinarily keep such interpretations to himself. A client can profit from the interviewer's insight only if it becomes also the client's insight, and this transfer cannot usually be made in so many words. The client must arrive at his own conclusions at his own pace. To be told that he feels anxiety, rejection, fear, and so on, will not help him. He must come to recognize the existence of such feelings himself with sufficient conviction so that he can voluntarily acknowledge their presence.

Once an interviewer realizes the existence of such underlying factors, he can often help his client to a recognition of them through discreet questions and comments, which include some element of interpretation. A client who is afraid to talk may be encouraged by a query such as "You are not quite sure I understand?" or by an interpretative question such as "You are afraid I will blame you as your mother has always done?" This latter question would be appropriate only if the client had already been able to express fairly freely his feeling of rejection.

In general, by encouraging a client to elaborate more fully, the interviewer helps him see for himself the relationships between the various things he has said. A man may talk freely about his hatred for his father and again about his "so-and-so" boss. A worker will have helped him understand, that is, to interpret the situation, if he can be led by further discussion to a recognition of the connection between these two hatreds. Often interpretation consists in opening lines of communication between two previously isolated compartments of thought.

In a few cases in which a secure relationship has been established between client and interviewer, we may wisely proffer a more direct interpretation. If a puny, precocious "mother's boy" looking longingly at a group of boys playing baseball remarks, "I don't like baseball," we may perhaps say gently, "You really mean that you would like to be out playing with them, but that they don't like you?" We would do this, however, only if we were sure that the boy felt certain the worker liked him. In this situation, the worker's expression of this thought for him might well be a relief. It would indicate to him that the worker really understands him and that it is not necessary for him to make painful admissions. If the worker had made such a comment early in his relationship with the boy, it would have appeared only as an accusation to be resisted. A sense of proper timing is important for an interviewer. Often what cannot be said earlier should be said later. With regard to many questions or remarks, it is not a matter of their goodness or badness but of their appropriateness at a given time.

Very often it is unnecessary ever to bring to a client's clear consciousness truths about himself of which the interviewer has become fully aware. It is important to remember that an interviewer's goal is seldom, if ever, to achieve a complete personality change in the client. As a result of changes in little ways and of slight modifications of attitude, people often come to be able to make their own decisions and work out their most pressing problems without having become consciously aware of the many factors that the interviewer may see in the situation.

6 What to look for in interviewing

It will be helpful for the reader to devise some method of studying interview records, his own or others. One helpful device is to use various symbols (checks, asterisks) to identify the more important aspects of interviewing to which attention has been called. The interviews of Part Two furnish good material for such an exercise.

For instance, with one symbol identify every recorded instance of the worker's activity, including gestures, questions, and comments. These passages may then be studied more readily to note the amount and kind of worker activity. Were the comments made to obtain further information, to encourage elaboration, to reassure, to indicate appreciation of the client's meaning, to restate and emphasize, or to refocus attention and redirect the course of the interview? Do they block or confuse the client or indicate understanding of him? Do they probe too deeply, proceed too fast, become argumentative or sarcastic, or are they sympathetic and appropriately timed?

We may also want to check and consider other aspects of interviewing. The following list is only suggestive. In addition to the items mentioned, we may want to examine an interview for certain specific points, such as mention of financial need, alcoholism, job experiences, and illness.

Association of Ideas

The phenomenon of free association is well known to the lay public. It has been publicized by William James under the name of stream of consciousness and by such fiction writers as James Joyce and Ernest Hemingway. It is worthwhile to be aware of its operation both in the client and in the interviewer. When the client mentions something, such as lying, divorce, a grandmother, there may be started in the interviewer a stream of association that has little to do with the client's feelings about these topics. The interviewer must recognize his own associations because otherwise they may operate unconsciously. That is, he may read into the client's problem feelings that he has but that the client may not have. On the other hand, if he listens for the client's own free association, he will gain many helpful clues about the things he is discussing. A father may be telling about his son's running away and, instead of continuing logically in this discussion of his son, may begin telling about his own youthful runaway escapades, indicating that to him his son's behavior is not a separate episode but is entangled with his own feelings carried over from his childhood. A mother may be telling about her inability to get along with her husband and switch suddenly to talking about her parents' separation when she was a child and her unhappiness and shame about this situation, thus indicating that her own current problems are not isolated but are connected in her mind with her parents' similar difficulties.

Shifts in Conversation

It is frequently difficult to understand why a client suddenly changes the topic of conversation. The reason often becomes apparent through study of what he was previously saying and the topic he begins to discuss. The shift may be an indication that he was telling too much and desires not to reveal himself further. It may be that he was beginning to talk about material that was too painful for him to pursue, perhaps too personal or too damning. On the other hand, it may be that what seems to the outsider as a shift in conversation is really a continuation, that in the unconscious of the client the two discussions have an intimate relationship. For instance, the interviewee may be discussing his difficulties with his foreman and suddenly begin discussing his childhood and the beatings his father gave him. The relationship in his own mind between his foreman and his father becomes clear. Or he may be discussing his mother and suddenly make a personal remark about the woman interviewing him, indicating that in his own mind she in some way reminds him of his mother.

Opening and Closing Sentences

The first words a client says are often of unusual significance. Even though they are about the weather, they may indicate some reluctance to accept the professional nature of the interview and a desire to keep it on a polite, social level. Frequently, the way in which a client first expresses his request gives the key to his problem and to his attitude about seeking help. He may start with "I don't suppose you can help me but . . ." or "I came because So-and-So sent me." The manner in which he states his problem always bears special study.

Concluding remarks are also noteworthy. Often a client's last remark indicates either his summing up of what the interview has meant to him or the degree to which his own forces have been mobilized for going ahead and working out his problem.

Recurrent References

In studying interviews we often notice a recurrent theme. A client repeatedly returns to a certain subject. This reference may be specific—a job, his need for money, his difficulties with his wife—or it may be more general. For example, we may detect throughout an interview repeated indications of difficulty with authority. The client complains about unjust treatment from his landlord, his father, his wife, and so on. Another person may reveal the theme of inability to express hostility. We may note that he is continually denying his own irritation. He starts to complain and then makes allowances.

Similar to repetition is the situation in which the client "talks in circles." He talks freely enough but does not move forward. He repeats the same ideas over and over. A man complaining about unfair treatment by his employer repeats and repeats his complaints, unswerved by the worker's explanation of his possible misinterpretations. A mother tells over and over again the story of her childhood or of difficulties with her husband. Such circularity presents a stumbling block to an interviewer. When we have become aware that such an impasse has been reached, it is necessary to devise ways of inserting something new into the ritual, thus breaking the circle and transforming it into a spiral. Here the interviewer's choice of a subject to insert is often guided by clues the client has given, perhaps some topic that has been mentioned before but not explained. If we have no clue, we may even have to make an insertion blindly, by trial and error. Questions such as "What would you like to do about it?" or "How would you like to have your husband act?" may stimulate the client to move into new and more profitable areas of discussion.

Inconsistencies and Gaps

We may note that the client's story is not unified. He often contradicts himself. His real meaning is not clear. Such behavior may indicate the operation of such internal pressure as guilt, confusion, or ambivalence.

A man may report that he finished high school and later tell how he has had to work full time since the age of ten. Another may seem sincere in his statement that he is bending all efforts to find a job and yet be unable to mention specific places where he has applied.

Or again, a client may tell a straightforward story but with unexpected gaps, areas in which the interviewer finds it impossible to elicit information. Frequently these areas are of particular importance. A man may carefully neglect to give any reasons for leaving his last job. A woman may discuss in great detail certain difficulties she has been having with the children but say nothing about her husband. The significance of such gaps and inconsistencies often becomes clearer through their cumulative force. One such occurrence may suggest a barely possible interpretation. But if ten others confirm this hypothesis, it is no longer a mere possibility but a probability.

Concealed Meaning

It is essential for the interviewer to accustom himself to listening to what his client means as well as to what he says. The little boy who does not like baseball is clearly suffering from "sour grapes" because he is friendless and unable to get along with children of his own age. Usually, however, the presence of concealed meaning is not as clear as in this instance, and often it is only with the most careful observation of slips of the tongue and attitudes and other clues that the interviewer can obtain any increased idea of the client's total meaning. An unmarried mother who protests that she does not even want to see the father of her baby again may be concealing her infatuation for him and her hurt that he has "left her in the lurch."

Sometimes clients practically announce the presence of concealed factors. A woman may say, "I don't know whether it's a job I'm worried about or other things." In a first interview it might be wise to concentrate attention on the job, but at a later stage it would be well to inquire about the "other things."

Several of the illustrative interviews in Part II contain excellent examples of concealed meanings which will be of interest to the reader to study.

7 Essential conditions of good interviewing

There are certain more concrete details in interviewing that should not be overlooked. Understanding and skill may be invalidated unless certain specific preparations are made for interviewing and certain precautions are taken. These may be listed under the general headings: (1) physical setting of the interview, (2) recording, (3) confidentiality, and (4) background knowledge of the interviewer.

Physical Setting

The physical setting of the interview may determine its entire potentiality. Some degree of privacy and a comfortable, relaxed atmosphere are important. The interviewee is not encouraged to give much more than his name and address if the interviewer seems busy with other things, if people are rushing about, if there are distracting noises. He has a right to feel that, whether the interview lasts five minutes or an hour, he has the undivided attention of the interviewer during that time. Interruptions and telephone calls should be reduced to a minimum. If the interviewee has waited in a crowded room for what seems to him an interminably long period, he is naturally in no mood to sit down and discuss what is on his mind. Indeed, by that time the primary thing on his mind may be his irritation at being kept waiting, and he frequently feels it would be impolite to express his annoyance. If a wait or interruptions have been unavoidable, it is always helpful to give the client some recognition that these are disturbing and that we can naturally understand that they make it more difficult for him to proceed. At the same

49

time, if he protests that they have not troubled him, we can best accept his statements at their face value; further insistence that they must have been disturbing may be interpreted by him as accusing, and he may conclude that we have been personally hurt by his irritation.

The length of the interview is, of course, so dependent upon the purpose of the interview that no optimum period of time can be fixed. In casework practice, however, it has been found that there is a great advantage in having the client know ahead of time that he will have a certain amount of time by appointment and that he may use it all or not as he wishes. In some agencies, interviews are as brief as fifteen minutes; in others longer periods are necessary. In general, it is seldom helpful to have the interview last more than an hour. Interviews lasting several hours exhaust both client and worker. They may indicate that the client has been trapped into telling more than he wanted to or that the interview has been inefficiently conducted so that too much time has been consumed in rambling. The fact that the client knows that his interview will terminate at a definite time may stimulate him to organize his material and present it concisely. Rather than have too long an interview, it is probably wise for the client to have time to digest and think over what he has said and what has been said to him. After the lapse of an interval permitting the client to reflect, a second interview will be more effective. It gives the client a greater sense of direction and security if he and the interviewer fix a definite time for the next appointment rather than leaving it to him to "come in again some day."

It is desirable for an interviewer to have time between interviews or during the day to think over each interview quietly and note any significant aspects of it. Although efficiency is important, it cannot be measured by the number of interviews conducted within a given period. Rather, efficiency in the interview relationship is proportional to the adequacy of understanding that is obtained, understanding that will make effective help possible. In the long run the greatest efficiency will be achieved by giving the client comfortable surroundings, undivided attention, and ample time to express himself during the interview.

The discussion thus far has assumed that most interviews will take place in an office. There are, of course, many instances in which interviews are of necessity or from choice conducted elsewhere, for example, in the home, at a person's place of employment, or in a school.

An office interview has obvious advantages because it provides opportunity for quiet and freedom from distracting interruptions. In addition, it is frequently preferred because people who seek out help for themselves are generally more likely to make use of it. The initiative required to leave the home and go to an office is often an indication of the client's ability to exercise some self-direction.

The fact that a client's willingness to leave home frequently indicates whether he is motivated does not mean, however, that we should make it a universal rule to refuse to visit clients. There are times when the client is unable to come to the office, and there are other times when he needs help and may later be able to bring himself to seek it actively. If the interviewer is rigid in his refusal to leave the office to offer his services, he may lose an opportunity to help when he is really needed. A person's failure to come into the office may have been due to his ignorance of the nature of casework service. In such a situation a "sample experience" of what the agency can offer, as demonstrated in a visit to the home, may alleviate his natural distrust of the unknown.

Recording

Among the many changes in social work practice in recent years is the substitution of tape recordings and audiovisual aids for the traditional written or dictated record of the process of an interview as recorded by the interviewer. Many agencies now require process recording only from students for purposes of supervision. In other agencies, usually ones with a large number of staff and sufficient equipment, students are also expected to use the mechanical aids. It is, of course, essential that clients' written permission to use these aids be obtained prior to the start of the interview and that the interviewer explain any professional use that will be made of the recorded interview.

However, some supervisors and many faculty in schools of social work prefer process records for most teaching purposes, along with tape recordings and audiovisual aids. Because students and beginning workers may be required initially to do process recording, the following suggestions may be helpful.

If an interviewer can set aside a few minutes immediately after each interview for jotting down full notes concerning it, he will be saved the necessity of making many notes during the course of the interview itself. It is always something of a question how much note taking during an interview is wise. There are usually certain factual things—names, addresses, dates, ages, places of previous residence or employment, and so on—that are normally written down as soon as they are mentioned. The interviewee regards it as perfectly natural for them to be noted and is not disturbed by the momentary pauses needed for writing them out.

If note taking goes beyond this point, however, the interviewee may easily feel that he does not have the interviewer's full attention and may be distracted from the normal progress of his account. Similarly, the interviewer's own participation may be interrupted or blocked by the exigencies of writing. Certainly when dynamic material is being revealed, the full attention of both interviewer and interviewee should be on the material itself. Even when an interviewer has an outline that must be filled in, he does not need to do so slavishly in one, two, three order. Often the answers to many questions come out naturally in the course of the interview and can be inserted later.

A beginning interviewer may need to make a number of notes as he goes along. An open notebook in which these may be jotted down unobtrusively is of great help. With practice, he finds that he can rely increasingly on mental notes rather than on written ones. Just a word or two in the already open notebook suffices to enable him to recall a whole phase of the conversation. With still more practice he finds that he can recall in amazing detail the full course of an interview.

Confidentiality

If a client is to feel it is safe to talk freely about his problems and what is troubling him, he has to be assured that whatever he reveals to the interviewer will be held in confidence or, at the very least, will not be misused. Preserving confidentiality is a responsibility that begins with the interviewer to whom the client communicates information but extends to all the personnel of the agency, including clerical staff and board members. Although state laws differ, most states do not accord the clients of social workers the protection of privileged communication. The client should be informed that, although such an eventuality is rare, the interviewer or the agency can not protect him from having the information he has given introduced as evidence in a judicial proceeding.

In earlier times, the case record was a written compilation of information about the client, with entries made by the caseworker and other professionals and placed in a folder in the agency files. Today, tape recordings, video recordings, and microfilms, are in common use as vehicles for documenting client and interviewer interaction and recording other material pertaining to the client's welfare. Consequently, these forms of record keeping must also be safeguarded. Many agencies have developed guidelines for recording practices and for defining to whom records may be made available.

Clearly, an important first element in preserving confidentiality is the physical safeguarding of all recorded materials. They should be kept under lock and key and accessible only to authorized personnel. They should not be removed from the agency for any reason. Equally important is the guarantee to the client that information about him will not be released to a third party without his informed consent. Informed consent means that he has been told what specific information about him has been requested, the person or agency to whom it will be released, and the uses to be made of it. Neither the interviewer nor the agency has the right to release information about the client for any purpose unless the client has given his consent in writing. Moreover, the client has the right to refuse to have his record, or information from it, used for any purpose except, of course, when the law compels its release.

Background Knowledge

There is a certain body of knowledge, some specific and some general, that is the responsibility of an interviewer to possess. The specific knowledge concerns the special purposes of the agency with which he is connected. An information clerk in a department store has to know where to direct anyone who wants an article sold in the store, but she would not be failing in her responsibility if she did not know the transportation schedule to a suburb. An interviewer in a public welfare agency has to know eligibility requirements but does not have to know, as an interviewer in an employment agency does, the skills required for various jobs. The amount of such specific information required is often considerable, but it varies greatly from one agency to another. On the other hand, there is a more general body of knowledge that every interviewer, no matter what agency he is associated with, should command. Such knowledge would include, at a minimum, the topics discussed in this book.

PART II
Illustrative
Interviews

A note on the interviews

The discussion of the following interviews is presented not as exhaustive but as suggestive. It will be helpful if the reader, before proceeding to the comments about each interview, will note in his own mind what he regards as the significant points of the interview in order to compare his views with the discussion that follows. In chapters 17, 18, 19, 20, and 22, where the interviews have been transcribed from tape recordings, the format may not make this suggestion feasible. The comments frequently follow immediately after the client's or the worker's statements. However, in the other chapters, the practice of the reader's pausing to consider what seems significant to him can be a useful method of studying an interview. If his own thinking does not follow the lines of this particular discussion, there is no reason for surprise or concern. There are many different ways in which these interviews might be considered, and each individual will inevitably make his own selection of certain points for special emphasis.

The primary objective is to learn to analyze interview material and to think constructively about it rather than merely to absorb "the story" in a passively receptive way. Any method that promotes this active thinking about the interviewee's problems and interviewing techniques is helpful. One method, that of checking the material for a number of crucial factors, has been mentioned in chapter 6.

8 "I'm bad and I do tell lies sometimes"

Helping a disturbed mother and an unhappy child

The Harris family record illustrates initial, individual interviews with the three members of the family: mother, adolescent daughter, and stepfather. The caseworker's skillful interviewing established a helping relationship that resulted in engaging the parents in an exploration of how best to help the daughter and ease the tension between her and her mother. The family consisted of Henry Harris, age forty, Gladys Harris, age thirty-three, and Betty, age thirteen.

Mrs. Harris was referred to the family service agency by Betty's high school teacher. She arrived one-half hour early for the appointment on August 3, accompanied by her daughter. She was a small, slender black woman, with bloodshot eyes, and a rigid posture. Her disturbed manner in the waiting room and her angry, authoritative attitude toward Betty led the worker to suggest that she see each of them separately. Betty, who kept her eyes fixed on her hands, tossed her head, saying that it was all right with her. Mrs. Harris agreed hesitantly.

The lengthy, disjointed interview with Mrs. Harris is summarized here to present relevant information. She talked continuously and gestured wildly. The worker had to interrupt several times to get answers to her questions. Mrs. Harris, however, would continue as if no interruption had occurred. Out of her circumstantial, rambling account, the chief concerns that emerged were that Betty never obeyed her, could not be trusted, and told lies. Mrs. Harris's brother, who lives across the street, frequently reported that Betty did not behave properly. Their neighborhood is "bad," and some of the neighborhood's girls have had illegitimate babies. Mrs. Harris became excited and smiled inappropriately as she detailed her fear of neighbors' derision and gossip if Betty became pregnant. Although Betty has denied ever having had intercourse, Mrs. Harris planned to take her for a physical examination.

Recently, Betty was seen kissing a friend of her stepfather, a thirty-five-year-old father of several children who lived in the same building. The Harrises took him to court and the judge advised them to move but they have been unable to find another apartment. The man has since moved.

Mr. Harris is Betty's stepfather. The Harrises were married six years ago. He is a "good" man and treats Betty well. She likes him and confides in him more than in her mother.

Mrs. Harris thinks Betty is like her father's family; his sister had an illegitimate child and he "lied, drank, and ran around."

Unlike her first husband's family, Mrs. Harris's family was hard-working, respectable, and had little to do with other people. She likes to keep her home clean, stay home, and go to church. She does not like to be with other people but she enjoys her work as a kitchen helper and likes her employers very much. Working helps to keep her mind occupied because worry about Betty has made her so nervous her doctor told her she was "run down."

Her plan was to send Betty to a boarding school to be disciplined. Betty accepted the plan after her mother told her otherwise she would end up in a reform school. Mrs. Harris stated that her husband was not in favor of this plan, believing that a child should be with her parents. Although she had come to request help in locating a school, Mrs. Harris felt confused and upset. She nodded in agreement at the worker's expressed understanding of her concern about having the responsibility of an adolescent daughter and uncertainty as to what a mother should do. Stating that a boarding school might be a solution, the worker explained that she needed to know more about how Mrs. Harris felt, as well as the reactions of her daughter and husband. Mrs. Harris agreed to their being interviewed but said that her mind was made up: A boarding school would discipline Betty, make her behave, and prevent her going to a reform school. The worker explained that she could not, on the basis of this one interview, share the responsibility for sending Betty away because Mrs. Harris had said she was not certain of her own reasons for doing so. Mrs. Harris became more receptive and, for the first time, looked at the worker. She commented that Betty's teacher had said that she was referring her to "a family agency— does that mean you want to keep families together?" She added *that was the way families should act with each other. The worker said that the agency tried to understand the situation of families like hers and help them solve the problems that were upsetting them. Mrs. Harris responded that perhaps it would be better if the worker talked to Betty and her husband and that it was all right to tell them that she thought a boarding school was the best solution. The worker explained that the interviews would be confidential, except for what each person agreed could be shared with the others. Mrs. Harris agreed that it was important to discuss the school plan and to know if Betty would feel it was punishment or would like it, because her attitude would affect the success of a school placement. She readily gave the necessary information for arranging an appointment with her husband. She stated she would wait for Betty, although they live near the office, because she does not trust her not to loiter for some time on the way home. She sat down in the waiting room and told Betty, "The lady wants to see you now." Her tone of voice was less authoritative and somewhat kinder than previously.*

Despite the client's agitated manner and confused talking, the worker succeeds in helping her focus on the need for more exploration of their situation by also seeing her daughter and husband. The client responds receptively when the worker does not deny the possibility of placement in a boarding school and explains why she cannot take immediate action to find a school. Mrs. Harris responds positively because her distress and worry about her daughter's future have been recognized and she can, to some extent, acknowledge her confusion regarding a solution. The worker, in asking for permission to discuss the school plan with the daughter and the husband, demonstrates that she respects the client's right to confidentiality, and prepares her to expect the same consideration to be shown in regard to the interviews with her family members. Mrs. Harris, feeling she has been understood, cooperates in arrangements for an interview with her husband and her calmer mood is shown in a less angry manner toward her daughter.

A significant fact that emerges in this interview, to be kept in mind in subsequent interviews, is that working outside the home is such a positive factor in Mrs. Harris's life. She enjoys her job and likes her employers even though she associates very little with other people. Despite her bizarre behavior and confused thinking, she evidently functions well on her job. It is important to consider what might happen to her precarious adjustment if she had to relinquish the area of her life where she seems to function well.

The interview with the daughter, as the worker was well aware, could present a serious obstacle to establishing real communication with the girl. Betty has had to wait alone for a long time, knowing that her mother is talking about her in negative terms to a stranger who may have some power or authority to affect her life. The worker can anticipate Betty's apprehensiveness and probable suspicion of her as another non-understanding adult—one perhaps already an ally of her angry, upset mother who wants to send her away. The worker knows she will have to allay Betty's suspicion and fear of her, demonstrate the sincerity of her interest in the girl and her parents, and make clear her wish to help them achieve a happier situation than now exists for them.

Interview with Betty—August 3

Betty came into the room. She was lighter in color than her mother, well-developed physically, big-boned, and very thin. Her eyes were almond shaped. When I introduced myself, she tossed her head and smiled rather superciliously. I said that I was sorry she had to wait. I imagined that she had questions about waiting and not being included in the interview with her mother, as she and her mother had intended. She did not care. I asked her if she knew why her mother had come here. She nodded, it was because she was bad. When I asked what she meant, she shrugged her shoulders and looked at her fingernails in silence. I said that it might help me to understand if she could tell me why she felt that she was bad. She tossed her head again, smiled, and again looked at her fingernails, but she did not speak. I explained why I wanted to see each of them alone. I could see that she was not very happy. Perhaps she was worried about what her mother had been telling me. She nodded and tears began to fall. I explained that I would not tell her what her mother had said, nor would I tell her mother what she said, unless we agreed together that certain things needed to be discussed in order to help in planning. She nodded her head, seemed more interested, but said nothing.

I said it would be hard for me to understand her and what was troubling her unless she tried to help me. I could see that she was not happy, and that she felt bad. She probably questioned how far she could trust me, especially because I had seen her mother first. Her tears stopped, and suddenly she looked at me and scowled. I responded that I was not going to assure her that she need not have feared trusting me—for to be assured she needed only to try me out.

Finally, Betty said in a whisper that she was bad, and that she did lie from time to time. In a louder tone, she said that she had a boyfriend, sixteen years old. Other girls were allowed to go with boyfriends in the evening, but she had not been allowed to do this. She liked the boy but he got her into trouble: they were caught kissing, and her uncle told her parents. Her mother did not believe that they had not had sexual intercourse.

She had lied, too, about staying away from school. She liked school, she did not have much homework, and school was easy for her. She had stayed away only half a day. When I asked what she thought were her reasons for lying, she said that it was because she was bad and because she was afraid her mother would beat her. She knew she should not lie. When questioned about the beating, she said that her mother did not really beat her very hard or very often. She ought to do her duties, they were not too much. Her mother only asked her to dust the house and do some marketing. If she had not lied, her mother would not now be sending her away from home. She started to cry, and then was silent.

I asked if she was unhappy about the school plan. She thought she should go away to school. I asked why. She cried again; she wanted to go to school to have friends. Her mother said that her friends in the neighborhood were not good. Some of them were bad; they were not married, had babies, and did not work. In a self-righteous tone of voice, she said that she would not want to be like her one friend, Helen, age fourteen, who stayed out late and whose mother drank. But she would like to have friends, and her mother had said that no one in the neighborhood was fit for her. She thought that some of them were nice. They liked to go to the drug-store and drink sodas, but her mother would not permit her to do this. Betty did not want to spend all of her time sitting in the house.

In talking with her further, I suggested that regardless of whose fault she felt it was, clearly the relationship between her and her mother was not a happy one. She nodded, crying hard. I was sorry she seemed so hurt. I wanted to understand and to see if I could help her. Would she like the relationship to be different? She nodded quickly. I said that I could not help her unless she helped me to understand her. She said that the relationship had never been very good, but it had become worse when she had started going out with boys two years ago. She had known the one she had told me about for a year. She had gone with him because all the girls had boyfriends. When she had invited him into the house, her uncle had seen him kissing her. Then she had not liked him any more because he had got her into trouble with her mother. It was all his fault. When I questioned this, she agreed that it was hers, too.

She wanted to go away to school because her mother wanted her to go and she would have friends there and could have more fun. I asked if she knew anything about a boarding school. A friend of hers was attending one in another state, and she was allowed to stay out in the evening and to have fun. I said that such schools usually had rules about coming in and going out. She said that she preferred going to a school in the North because they had better educational opportunities for people like her. She hesitated. I suggested that she was speaking about opportunities for blacks and, because I was a white person, perhaps it was not easy for her to tell me about herself. She nodded assent. I thought it might be like my relationship with her mother, that is, she would not know whether she could trust me until she had more experience with me. She looked up with a smiling face and appeared more receptive.

She felt that there would be less unhappiness for everyone if she were to go to a boarding school. She did not want to wait until her mother would have to send her to reform school. I asked her why she thought about that. Her mother had said that if boarding school failed and if she continued to lie, or to go with boys and girls in the neighborhood who were not any good, the only thing left would be reform school. She looked down at her fingernails, began to pick them, and tears came again. I asked if this place seemed like a court to her, since she had mentioned reform school. She nodded. I explained that we were in no way connected with the court. We tried to help families, such as hers, to be happy together. If, for some reason, this was not possible, then we had to help them find the best solution so that all of them would feel happier. Did she think that she would be happier at school than at home? She shook her head. Would she like to visit home? She shook her head, crying harder. She would not like to visit, because it would make her too homesick. When I asked for whom, she did not know.

Because she appeared so upset, I inquired about her health. It was all right. She slept well but did not have a good appetite. Usually she was not hungry at mealtime, nor did she eat between meals. She had lost six pounds in the last month.

Because her mother wanted her to go away I asked Betty how Mr. Harris felt about this plan. She brightened considerably for the first time. She would have gone to school long ago, but her stepfather had not wanted her to go. He did not want to put her out of the house. Henry (she called her stepfather by his first name), felt that a child's place was with the parents. She liked him very much, found it easier to talk to him than to her mother. He trusted her more. She cried again and picked at her fingernails. Because our time was up, I told her that I would like to see her stepfather and asked her what she thought about this. She nodded, still crying. I asked her what she wanted me to say to her mother and stepfather. She said to tell them that she wanted to go away. I said I would tell them that, but I would like to add that I thought that she was not happy over the decision. How would she feel about my saying that? She looked at her fingers again and nodded. I told her that I would say only that—unless there was something else she wanted me to say. There was nothing else. I explained that this was not a placement agency, and that I would have to refer her elsewhere for school placement if the family wanted that. If she and the family should decide that she was to remain at home, would she like to try to understand why she and her mother were not happy together in order to see if anything could be done about it? She nodded. I assured her no plan would be made here without her participation. I was sorry to see her so unhappy, and I hoped I could help her.

The worker immediately apologizes for Betty's having to wait and gives her an opportunity to ask questions about being excluded from the interview with her mother. Betty, who initially smiled rather superciliously, denies any concern and the worker then asks if she knows why her mother came to the office. Betty indicates it was her "bad" behavior but cannot elaborate on this statement. The worker explains why she decided on separate interviews and tells Betty that she sees her unhappiness and suggests that she may be worried about what her mother has said about her. Betty agrees and begins to cry. The worker explains that each interview is confidential, except for whatever Betty agreed needs to be shared with her parents in order to help in planning.

The worker's flat statement that she would not reveal what Mrs. Harris said in her interview is poorly phrased and could have made Betty even more fearful. A comment that her mother was concerned about her, as Betty knows, and wants help in planning for her, would have been more reassuring. When the worker is specific about obtaining Betty's permission to report to her mother, Betty, who has been crying, does not reply.

The worker then asks for Betty's help in understanding what is troubling her and recognizes her fear of trusting the worker. She suggests that Betty can be reassured only by testing the worker—trying her out. Betty responds by telling of her "badness": occasional lying and kissing a boyfriend. She states that she lied because she was "bad" and because she was afraid if she told the truth her mother would beat her as she sometimes did.

As Betty gains confidence in the worker, who is not critical of her and whose manner and comments demonstrate sincere concern for her, she reveals her need for friends and her mother's rigid opposition to her having any companionship with her peers in the neighborhood. Betty says that she wants to go away to school because her mother wants her to, and also because she sees it as an opportunity to have the friends and fun she does not have now. When she refers to wanting to go to a school in the North because of "better educational opportunities," the worker recognizes that Betty is speaking about opportunities for blacks and because the worker is white, it may be hard for her to tell the worker about herself. Betty nods assent, smiles and looks more receptive when the worker comments that Betty could not trust her until she had more experience with her.

When Betty refers to reform school, the worker senses her concern about the agency's possible connection with the court and reassures her that there is no connection, but that the agency tries to help families feel happier.

At the first mention of her stepfather, Betty looks happier and says that she thought she would have been sent away to school long ago except for him. She can talk more to him and feels he trusts her. She begins to cry during the discussion of going away but says that she wants the worker to tell her parents that she wants to go away to school. She agrees that the worker can add that she does not think Betty is happy about the plan. The worker explains that the agency is not a placement agency, and reassures Betty that no plan would be made there without her participation.

This interview well illustrates how a sensitive interviewer, anticipating the reactions of an unhappy adolescent, threatened with being sent away from her home, is able to alleviate some of her fear and suspicion of a worker whom she has just met and of the agency which she knows her mother has come to for help in placing her. The worker's understanding of what the child is experiencing enables Betty to reveal her feelings of being "bad" (as she knows her mother perceives her) and to "confess" her occasional lies to prevent beatings by her mother. Because of her fear of being sent to a reform school, as forecast by her mother, she is prepared to agree to a boarding school although she does not want to leave her home. Knowing Betty's real feeling, the worker holds out the possibility of working with the family to improve the relationship between her and her mother to which Betty quickly agrees. The worker ends the interview with an empathic statement about Betty's unhappiness and an expression of her hope to be able to help her.

Interview with Mr. Harris—August 7

Mr. Harris was half an hour early, but I was able to see him at once. He was a small man with a direct manner. He said that his wife had misunderstood the time. She did this whenever she was upset, and she was very upset about Betty. He thought it best to make plans for a boarding school. I said his ideas were important in our planning. He thought that Betty did not like the idea of school. With both of them working, she was left to her own resources. Her mother gave her plenty to do, housework and marketing, just to keep her out of mischief. She wanted to run in the streets with other children in the neighborhood. Her mother did not think that they were the right sort of children.

I said it was important to me to know what he thought. At first he was silent, and then said that he felt Betty had to have friends. She needed to be kept busy, but housework was not the only way to do it. His wife was so neat that she was never satisfied; she spent endless time cleaning the house. He shook his head and smiled. His wife should stay home and supervise Betty, he earned good money. He had worked steadily since they had arrived from the South.

I commented that he had never been married before and I wondered how he felt about the responsibilities of a family. He stated that his wife had been honest; he had known about Betty and he had no complaints about his responsibilities. He then asked me rather suspiciously if his wife had said he objected; he thought she might have because I had asked him. I replied that I was just trying to understand. He had told me that he had never married before, and now he was faced with the responsibilities of a wife and an adolescent stepdaughter. He seemed more receptive, nodded, but said nothing. I told him, as I had told his wife and Betty, that everything he said to me was confidential. He could say whatever he wished to the two others about what had occurred here; I would tell each of them only what he and I agreed might help. He nodded.

He expressed the feeling that a child's place was in the home. Betty would have been sent to a school before, if it had not been for him. Gladys expected too much of her; she wanted immediate obedience. She was afraid of what people would say. She listened to her brother too much. She was not unkind, but did not understand what to expect from an adolescent girl. The girl had to have friends. Gladys was good, hardworking, and a constant church-goer. He did not care too much for church. Gladys accused Betty so that she *either lied or refused to talk. He got further with Betty by not being judgmental until he had the facts. Betty's word was as good as anyone else's, until proved otherwise. He must have proof, not rumors. Gladys was afraid that Betty would get into sex trouble and bring disgrace on them. To be truthful, she would fly off the handle and beat Betty. He tried to stop her; this only made Betty more sly and then she would not tell anything. If Betty had a bad name without deserving it, she might do what Gladys feared—get into trouble with boys.*

I asked what he thought about Betty. He replied that she was not able to withstand suggestions of others; she wanted affection, was bright, and had never been in serious trouble, as far as he knew. The change in Betty's behavior occurred when his friend had made advances toward her. It was not her fault. Mrs. Harris, however, had become upset. He gave the same account of this episode as his wife had.

Since coming here, however, Betty seemed more serious and her behavior had improved. She went to church with her mother and was trying to please her. She was also more cheerful about household tasks. I wondered what had caused this change. He thought it might have been my conversation with her. I asked him what he felt was the reason the family had come here. He knew the school had sent a note for Gladys because she had been upset several weeks ago. Other children usually tore up a note or signed it themselves; Betty was truthful about it. Her mother had told her that she was going to bring her here to find a boarding school as the teacher had suggested. Betty had begged her mother not to do this, because she was afraid of being sent to a reform school. Mrs. Harris had frequently threatened Betty with this, hoping that the threat would result in obedience. Threats were not right for her. He had told them both that Mrs. Harris could not send Betty to a reform school for what she had done. It was not real trouble. Betty did not lie to him, but she did lie to her mother.

I asked how his protection of Betty and his differing opinions about her affected his relations with his wife. They did not; he and his wife never fought over her. He wanted me to understand that Betty was the responsibility of Mrs. Harris. Betty had never been responsible for any differences between them. Gladys did go after him occasionally, for example, when he was not neat enough. He would just leave the house; he would not take accusations as Betty had to do. By this he meant accusations of running around, which he did not do. If Gladys were to accuse him of that, he would leave her.

I explained that, from my interview with his wife and from what he had told me, I was concerned about her. He nodded and said that she was very nervous. She was good-hearted, but worked too hard. She did not eat and was rundown physically. She had been nervous ever since he had known her, and she never had friends. She always felt that the neighbors were watching her, however, there was no special person about whom she felt this. She was also very religious. After beating Betty, she cried and was quite upset. She was also very sensitive. She talked constantly, and it was hard to interrupt her. They did not have much of a chance to be with each other because of different working hours.

He was not sure about a boarding school for Betty. I asked about this, because at first he had believed it best. He asked if it would provide an opportunity for Betty to learn a lot, to have supervision, and to meet the right kind of friends. I was not sure. Because he himself was not sure, perhaps he could raise some questions about it. Both Mrs. Harris and Betty had said that I could tell him that they both had requested the school plan. I had been concerned about the decision, because Betty had cried and I felt she was not happy about it. Mr. Harris did not really think she was. She felt that it was a punishment for what she had done, and for being thought of as bad.

I wondered if attending school would benefit her if she were unhappy. He was silent; he then said he thought school seemed best, because he did not want more trouble between Mrs. Harris and Betty. However, he thought if she could stay away from school for half a day as she had done, she might run away entirely if sent to a boarding school. She had never threatened it, but after an argument with Gladys, when he had walked out of the house, Betty had said that sometimes she had felt like doing it.

Betty had explained to her mother and to him that we had nothing to do with court, that we wanted to help people to be happy. He would like to talk this over again with Betty and with his wife, as we had done. If Betty was not happy about it, and could not regard school as an opportunity, he did not want to send her. He did not care so much about the expense, but he would not take the responsibility for a decision; Gladys could do it alone. If Gladys asked me to look into the matter of schools, I should go ahead and she could decide. I wondered if Mrs. Harris's and Betty's nerves could stand much more. Mr. Harris said that he would help in the decision if Betty wanted the plan. If not, Gladys and Betty could decide what their nerves could stand. Anyway, they had not really talked it over. Gladys had become excited after the episode with the boy and had marched Betty here. He would like to talk it over with them, then discuss it further with me. I asked him if I might tell his wife this because I was going to see her later that day. I intended to raise some of the same questions with her. He agreed.

The worker's description of Mr. Harris's direct manner is shown in his immediately stating what action he thought best; however, he needs a second comment from the worker about the importance of his ideas to encourage him to reveal his understanding of Betty's needs and his differing attitude from his wife's. The worker's question about how he felt about his responsibility appears to be threatening to him: he asks if his wife had said that he objected. The worker in this exchange seems less sensitive; she does not clarify that his wife had no complaints about him but replies she is "trying to understand." This comment seems to reassure Mr. Harris but his momentary suspiciousness probably would not have occurred had the worker's question been phrased in more empathetic terms rather than a question which felt to the client like an accusation. The worker next introduces the idea of confidentiality in a way that seems poorly phrased and also poorly timed, as it might cause him to wonder further what his wife had said about him. Mr. Harris apparently accepts it, however, and readily elaborates on his thinking about the reasons for the tension between his wife and Betty, volunteering additional information about their interaction, demonstrating his ability to understand both, and his attempts to intervene. The interview proceeds with an easy give and take between the worker and Mr. Harris who thoughtfully cooperates in the worker's exploration of the family relationships. Her concern for Mrs. Harris's emotional state is echoed by his, which is leading him to think a boarding school may be the solution. He decides that he wants to talk it over again with his wife and Betty and, if his wife decides to go ahead with the plan, it would be her responsibility for the decision if Betty continues to feel she is being punished. He expresses a wish to talk again with the worker.

The following is a summary, with an excerpt, from the interview later that day with Mrs. Harris. There was considerable repetition of the discussion in her previous interview but she indicated more ambivalence about sending Betty away. Although she and Betty had agreed on the plan, she wanted the worker's opinion.

Interview with Mrs. Harris, August 7—an Excerpt
I suggested she was feeling pressed and that perhaps she was not sure of her decision. She nodded and her eyes filled with tears. I

expressed concern about her and about what her indecision and feelings of responsibility for Betty were doing to her. Weeping, she again asked what I thought. I said that I wanted to help her with the decision. I had questioned her, Betty, and Mr. Harris as to what they hoped from schooling, and I wanted to raise some additional questions with her.

I was not sure that school would meet their expectations. She said that Betty had been better since she had come here; had gone to church, and was also staying in the house. She asked what I thought of Betty. I suggested that she might be concerned about my interview with Betty. She answered that she was a funny child, she took likes and dislikes to individuals. She had told her that she liked me, and wanted to bring me a gift. I wondered what she thought about this. She felt I could help her with what to do about Betty. Betty had told her that she wanted to go to boarding school, and that she would not want to come home because she would be too lonesome.

Mrs. Harris's employer had told her that her daughter's place was at home. She cried hard, and I waited until she was calm. I said I thought it might be hard for her, because so many people were advising such different things; her brother was in favor of her plan, while her employer was against it, and she herself feared what neighbors might say if Betty should get into trouble. She said that she wanted to do what was right, and she was not sure what this was. Did I think Betty wanted to go? I said Betty had told me that I could say that she wanted to go. However, because she had cried and seemed unhappy, I thought it best to let her mother and Mr. Harris know that in spite of what she had said, she seemed unhappy over it. Mrs. Harris nodded and seemed calmer. If Betty continued as she was doing now, boarding school would not be necessary. Mrs. Harris said that she had thought of it when they had gone to court. She began to talk in a compulsive fashion, waving her hands and smiling inappropriately. She returned to her former complaints about Betty.

As the interview continued, the worker interrupted Mrs. Harris's complaints, again recognizing her uncertainty, her anger with Betty, and the great tension that the worker wanted to help lessen. Mrs. Harris cried as she explained her need to work and her fear that the worker would say that she should stay home to supervise her daughter, which she could not bear. Mr. Harris had suggested this plan. The worker reassured her that she was not going to suggest any such change at that time. She knew Mrs. Harris felt more comfortable working and the worker did not want to do anything to cause her more discomfort.

Realizing how much Mrs. Harris feared what others might say about her, the worker stated that she could understand that she might be worried about the interviews with Betty and Mr. Harris. Other people may think that she should give up her job but she knew she could not and the worker understood how important the job was to her. Mrs. Harris then readily agreed to discuss her health condition and worries in future interviews. I emphasized that it was important for all three of them to feel comfortable about the decisions they made.

In this second interview, the worker's empathic feeling again reaches Mrs. Harris despite her agitation, so that she can freely express her fear of having to give up her job to stay home and supervise her daughter.

Mrs. Harris tearfully repeats her need to work and, in a sense, she pleads with the worker not to suggest she give up her job in order to give Betty more supervision. With this further confirmation of the value of work to Mrs. Harris's functioning—she "could not bear" to give up her job—the worker assures her that she understands her need and will not suggest a change to cause her such discomfort. Realizing the worker's sincere concern for her welfare, Mrs. Harris readily agrees to the suggestion that in future interviews they focus on the condition of her health as well as her many other worries.

The worker offers to call some schools for information so that if, after discussion, the three agreed that a boarding school is the best solution, they can contact the schools themselves. Although this offer may seem premature, the worker may have made it to demonstrate to Mrs. Harris that she was keeping an open mind and respecting their right to decide for themselves. It may also, however, have confused Mrs. Harris as to what the worker was really recommending to them.

August 9

Mr. Harris telephoned asking for an appointment to discuss the school situation so that there would be no misunderstanding. Both he and his wife wanted to hold up school plans and wanted me to know what they were thinking.

August 14

Mrs. Harris was fifteen minutes early. She wanted to wait for Mr. Harris because they both agreed that it was best to discuss the decision together. He stated that it had been his idea for me to see them together. *He wanted me to understand why he did not want to take responsibility for the decision to send Betty to school. Some of the questions he and I raised together had started him thinking, and he had a long and serious talk with Betty. He understood young people; they have to be treated like human beings. All children need to be respected.* His wife interrupted him to say that Betty could not be treated in this way because Betty thought she knew more than anyone else. Mrs. Harris began her obsessive talking and complaining about Betty.

He cut in brusquely, saying that he knew Betty was not perfect. Maybe he made mistakes, too. He could not believe that Betty was all bad. He knew she was not happy at home and had said that she wanted to go to school. He had wanted to know why. She was afraid of reform school. She had cried while talking with him. She did not think of school as an opportunity to be good, but as a punishment because she was not wanted at home. She wanted an opportunity to be good at home. He would be willing to send her if she had a different idea about it.

Mrs. Harris interrupted. She could pay for the schooling. He said that it was not a question of money alone. He had agreed to this plan because his wife had become upset. He added, suppose Betty did not like the school and ran away—then what? She might get into more trouble and it would not be the school's fault. If she felt happy about going then she would do well. He would have no part in this plan.

I said that I was interested in his reactions to the plan, but Mrs. Harris's feelings were also important. Mrs. Harris said that if Betty should run away she would have to go to reform school. Mr. Harris became angry. He could not understand why she was always thinking of reform school. Betty had done nothing bad.

Mrs. Harris said that she was not able to stay at home with Betty. The couple began interrupting each other, but Mr. Harris was more gentle with his wife than he had been. I said that I had called one school but there were no openings. I could give them a list of other schools to call and then they could decide for themselves. I asked them why they had let this go so late. Mrs. Harris said that she had thought that Betty would be better after the teacher had referred her here. She should have placed her in a summer camp. Mr. Harris agreed, they could have seen how Betty liked being away from home and how she could behave. I asked if they had ever tried sending her away from home. Mrs. Harris had sent her every summer for six years to relatives in another state. She had not been satisfied with the supervision given her.

Mr. Harris thought it would not do to make school plans now. Maybe I could suggest ways to help Betty be happier if they decided to send her away. He knew that all of this would take time. Meanwhile, he asked if I could help. Maybe there were places for her to go after school and on Saturdays. I said that I would like to help. Perhaps I could be of more assistance when I had better understanding of the real problem. For instance, why did Mrs. Harris feel under such pressure? Perhaps I could help relieve this pressure. However, Mrs. Harris might feel that school was the only solution. Her feelings were very important. Mrs. Harris said that she had not been sure. I realized that this had been hard on her. I was concerned about how much pressure she could stand. Both nodded. Mr. Harris then suggested that I see Betty, and also see Mrs. Harris. She, however, expressed worry about the kind of supervision Betty would get if she stayed home. Mr. Harris interrupted to say that this subject could be discussed in greater detail at other times.

Mr. Harris's positive reaction to his first interview with the worker is evidenced by his taking the initiative in requesting a joint interview for him and his wife, and then in assuming the lead in postponing precipitate action in regard to sending his stepdaughter away. In the presence of the worker his understanding of children is expressed freely, despite his wife's lack of agreement with his thinking about Betty. He firmly holds to their need to postpone a decision, and asks the worker to help Betty find acceptable social activities. He is emphatic in his refusal to support a plan to send Betty away as long as she considers it a punishment.

When the worker is supportive of his reactions and yet calls attention to his wife's feelings, Mr. Harris again shows understanding of her condition, despite their arguments in this interview. Thus the focus for future interviews is directed toward needing to understand Mrs. Harris's pressures, a focus the worker has been articulating in the previous interviews. Mr. Harris supports the need for continued help for his wife and Betty and suggests deferring further discussion of his wife's concern about supervision of Betty until future interviews.

In the next interview, Mrs. Harris reported Betty's continuing satisfactory behavior; she was doing more chores at home and attending church.

Mrs. Harris's account of an accident to a neighbor's child which included her dreams about it led into a description of occasional "spells" when she goes into a sleep-like state and loses track of time. She sometimes sees Betty's father and hears his voice telling her she must take care of Betty. Her husband had died a few days after a stroke; she was in a state of shock and went into a medical hospital. She had never had psychiatric care but often thought she should.

Mrs. Harris, in answer to the worker's query about her refusal to permit her daughter to attend movies (except only occasionally), dance, or play cards with her girlfriends, gave an account of her own deprived childhood. Her mother died when she was six, and her father died a year later. She and her nine-year-old sister then lived with their grandmother who was "very strict." Sometimes the sisters lived with and worked for neighbors for their room and board, moving from one house to another. When she was twelve, her grandmother died and an aunt took the girls into her home. There they worked long hours each day doing large bundles of laundry. They never had time to play. When she was sixteen, she met her first husband, a railway employee, nineteen years older than she. A few years later, when she was two months pregnant, he married her and took her to live in his mother's home.

In later interviews, Mrs. Harris reported feeling less pressured. As she came to recognize that Betty would listen to her stepfather's suggestions, she felt relieved of the need to watch Betty constantly. She responded to the worker's understanding of her great feeling of responsibility for her daughter. She felt better about keeping Betty at home, stating that she knew she would still have worried about her if she were at a boarding school. She agreed that examining her many feelings of pressure was helping her cope with less distress for herself and less tension for her family.

The above partial summary of subsequent interviews is presented to illustrate how skillful interviewing can direct focus on to the family member who seems most in need of help with beneficial results for the whole family. The worker's goal of helping the clients recognize the need for such a focus is achieved despite the difficulty of communication in the beginning interviews with an upset woman, agitated in behavior, rambling and confused in speech.

The husband's understanding of his wife and stepdaughter and his ability to express his thinking clearly and with conviction were important supports for the worker's attempts to forestall a possibly destructive plan for the child. At the same time she involved the parents in further consideration of plans for the child's need of friends and social activities with her peers, and exploration of the mother's need for relief from her distress and pressures.

Clearly, the worker's ability to understand each family member's feelings expressed in supportive, empathic comments and her thoughtful questions led to their gaining trust in her help, and in their acceptance of the need for a continued contact with her.

The mother's opportunity to describe her own harsh childhood does much to explain her unawareness of her daughter's need for peer relationships and social activities outside the home. The revelation (in such a low voice it was barely audible) that she had become pregnant before marriage could be the basis of her concern for a similar fate in her daughter's future. What a great sense of relief it must have been for her to share "the terrible thing that happened—such shame," and to realize her listener did not express shock, disapproval, or rejection of her, but continued to be a truly trustworthy person who was concerned about her and her feelings.

9 "I just stick it out the best I can"

Living with loneliness and illness

One of the frequent requests made of social workers in a hospital setting is to interview a patient to obtain personal history and other information on his current situation that will enable the doctors and nurses to enlarge their understanding of the patient, his emotional make-up, habitual ways of coping with problems, and the problems and resources in his environment that can hinder or aid in his recovery. The interview that follows illustrates how a beginning worker fulfilled this function. She obtained considerable information that would be helpful in the medical planning, and at the same time, established a relationship with a depressed man, living an isolated, lonely existence, who responded to her interest and agreed to a continuing contact with her.

Leslie Stevens was referred to Social Service during the health-team ward rounds on September 27. It was thought that a social evaluation was needed because the patient seemed depressed, and because he lived alone and would not be able to take care of himself upon discharge in his present weak physical condition. It was known that Mr. Stevens had lived with his brother until about one year ago when the brother died, and Mr. Stevens became depressed as a result. The purpose of my interview was to talk to Mr. Stevens and see how he was getting along on his own, investigate the reports of depression, talk about his feelings, how he passes his days, and investigate the need for homemaker services upon discharge.

Mr. Stevens's diagnosis was chronic obstructive pulmonary disease. I talked to his intern, Dr. Armstrong. He stated that there was serious lung disease, blood in the stool, and stomach distress that were currently being investigated. The ward rounds team reported a very weakened physical condition and an inability to get out of bed. The patient also had glaucoma and could not see well. Nurses' notes indicated Mr. Stevens's lethargy and unwillingness to get out of bed—even for linen change.

Mr. Stevens was a seventy-seven-year-old white male, a native of the city. He was single (never married) and lived alone. He was a retired elevator operator.

Interview—October 1

Mr. Stevens was a small, thin man who looked as if he were just "skin and bones." His face was very drawn and his skin was so close to his skull that it appeared almost shrunken. His eyes also seemed sunken. His arms were almost completely bruised, as if so many blood tests had been done that the blood had collected under the surface of his skin. One of the reasons his face looked so drawn was that he had no teeth. His hair was neatly combed, but he needed a shave. Mr. Stevens seemed friendly and responsive. He was somewhat hard of hearing. I had to speak louder and repeat myself many times throughout the interview.

I introduced myself to Mr. Stevens by giving my name and saying that I was a social worker for the hospital. Mr. Stevens asked me to repeat my name and it took several repetitions before he got it straight. He smiled and seemed very amused that we shared the same first name.

I asked if it was all right if I sat down and talked with him a little while. He said "Sure," and turned on his side in the bed to face me. I told him again that I was a social worker for the hospital and I had come to talk to him about how he was getting along. I asked if he had anything in particular he wanted to talk about, any problems or anything? Mr. Stevens stated that he really did not have any problems. He said that they were treating him good here, just trying to help him get better. He wanted to get better too, so he tried to cooperate with them as much as he could.

I told him that I had tried to see him earlier that day, but that I was told he was having some tests. (I said this because I thought it might help to start talking about the hospital and the past few days before opening up to something else.) Mr. Stevens said that he had had many tests done, and he did not know why. He said he knew people were trying to help him get better, and they were helping his breathing. But he did not know why they kept giving all these tests. I asked him if he had talked to the doctor about the tests. He replied that he had not. People were so busy that he did not want to annoy them and he knew they were just trying to make him better. (Dr. Armstrong had told me they were investigating blood in the stool. I had asked him if the patient knew this and he had said yes. Evidently, Mr. Stevens did not know it or for some other reason did not mention it.) Mr. Stevens then went on to elaborate on the testing procedures he had been through that morning. He stated that the worst part for him was just lying on those hard tables; they were so hard on his bones. I responded that it must be very uncomfortable for him. (He is so thin that an unpadded table would be painful to him.) Yes, he said, it was. He stated that doctors had to "knock him out" for the tests that morning and that he was still tired from that a little.

I told Mr. Stevens that I might be able to help him with making plans to go home. He said that he already had a social worker who helped him at home. I asked what things she helped him with. He described the services. He had homemaker service once a week (every Tuesday) and Meals on Wheels, both of which his social worker had obtained for him. He had not started Meals on Wheels yet—he was just about to start when he came to the hospital. I asked Mr. Stevens if he had been cooking for himself. He said that he cooked something for breakfast, like a scrambled egg or oatmeal, or ate cold cereal. He went out everyday to eat lunch. I asked if he cooked supper for himself. He said that he could not cook anything. I then asked if he had anything to eat after lunch. He said he made a sandwich or maybe warmed up a can of something.

I asked Mr. Stevens what the homemaker did for him. He said that she cleaned and went to the store for him. I asked if he ever needed her to come more than one day a week. He said that he did not want her to come more often because he lived in only one room and there was not much to do. Plus, with a stranger, you really do not have much to say to each other, nothing in common. He said that it might get lonely sometimes, but he would rather not have anyone than a stranger sitting around with nothing to do. Besides, he said, when it was hot he liked to sit around in his shorts, and he could not do that with a woman around could he? (I will, at another time, comment on his mention of loneliness, but I wanted him to tell me more about his everyday life first).

I asked him what he did on the days his homemaker did not come. Did he manage all right on those days? He replied that he got along fine, adding that the superintendent's wife from one flight down often helped him. She visited him regularly, shopped for him, and sometimes cooked and brought him food. He told me that she was the one who called to get him to the hospital. I asked what had happened to make him come to the hospital. He said that he had been "so bad" lately that he could hardly catch his breath or walk. He even had a hard time standing up to shave. The superintendent's wife came to see him and said, "You are too sick to be here like this." She called the doctor and asked his niece to take him to the hospital. I inquired if the niece who came to get him was Marian (the name recorded on his admission form). He said, yes, Marian was his niece who lived in a nearby town. He told me that she visited him in the hospital once a week, not coming every day because she worked and lived too far away. She always telephoned every night. I told him that it sounded as if he had a lot of people looking in and checking on him. He agreed that he did. He also added that he had lived in the same neighborhood all his life, and everyone there knew him.

I asked Mr. Stevens to tell me about his daily routine, starting with getting up and getting dressed every morning. He said that he made a point to get up and dressed even if it took him thirty minutes or an hour. Then he prepared something for breakfast. After that, he usually sat down and read the newspaper or a magazine, and smoked. He said he smoked a lot—he just could not stop even though he knew it was bad for him. He had stopped drinking, but he could not stop smoking. He went on to say that he would lie down to rest often, but would not stay in bed too long. He said that he knew it was important to get out and exercise or he would get even weaker. Therefore, he made a point of getting out at least an hour or two every day, but lately he had been unable to do that because he could hardly walk. Before, when he went out for lunch, he stayed out for several hours. He usually returned to his apartment, around three-thirty in the afternoon. Then he sat and rested, and later fixed himself something to eat. I asked if he watched television or listened to the radio. He responded that he did not like television, especially in the daytime. He liked the sports in the afternoons and sometimes watched a program at night.

I said that he had been telling me a lot about the things he did and how he managed things and asked if he would tell me something about the way he felt. He asked what I meant. I clarified my question by bringing up the fact that he had mentioned feeling lonely a little while before. He told me he did feel lonely sometimes ever since his brother had died. At the mention of this, he started to cry. He did not actually break into sobbing, but his voice trembled, his chin quivered, and tears came to his eyes, and a few spilled out the corners. He did not turn away, or bring his hands to his face, or seem embarrassed at all. He kept right on talking. It was as if an emotional wave had come over him suddenly at the thought of his brother and passed in just a matter of a few seconds. I said that it must hurt him very much to have lost his brother. He agreed; they had lived together for so long and had done everything together. I said that he must miss him very much and feel lonely without him. He said he did, and continued immediately that his niece wanted him to stay with her. I asked how he felt about that, would he like to stay with her? He responded that he could not stay there; there was nothing he would like better, but he just could not. I asked what made him feel that he could not. He replied that he just thought he would be interfering too much in her family, and would get in their way. I asked what he meant. He said that she had children, and he might annoy them; her husband might think he "took up too much" for his niece. In addition, his niece's elderly mother lived with them, and he would just be too much. He continued, saying that he got sick sometimes and that he did not like to be with anyone when he was sick. I asked him to explain what he meant and he said that sometimes at night he coughed a lot, sometimes coughed up "stuff," and that he could not be doing that at someone else's house. He said that he got up at night to get a soda or a candy bar, and that that might disturb them or they might not have what he wanted. He added that years ago he used to stay with them every weekend. He had helped the husband with work on the house, and he did not feel bad then because he was helping them.

I responded that it seemed as if he thought he would be an annoyance or in the way, and would feel bad about staying with them if he could not do something in return for them. He agreed. I asked if he had ever talked to his niece about the way he felt. He had not. I suggested that maybe he could talk to her about it, since it seemed as if he would like to stay with her, and that she wanted him to because she had asked him several times. He replied that he knew she wanted him to, and that she meant it, but that he just could not. I said that he felt he just could not live with anyone else. He replied that he did not mean live with them; they did not ask him to live with them, only to stay for awhile. (I had assumed that he had meant live with them.) He went on to say that he did not think he could ever live with anyone. I asked why. He said it was as he told me before—he would just interfere in someone's business, and he did not like that; he got sick and needed to be alone. He told me about a time he visited his niece and planned to spend the night, but he started feeling sick and came back to his apartment.

I asked what he did in his apartment when he got sick. He said he just lay down and "stuck it out" the best he could. Another wave *of emotion, as he had experienced when speaking of his brother, passed over him. This time he did turn away from me, on his back, for a moment. He faced me again and said that he did not want me to think he was turning away from me: His eyes got fuzzy sometimes looking into the light (I was sitting so that he was facing the window as he faced me) and he was tired from being "knocked out" that morning. He then began to elaborate on what he could or could not see.*

I ended the interview by saying that if he was tired, I would not keep him from resting but would be back to visit him again. I said that perhaps we could talk some more about anything else he wanted to discuss. I told him that I was available to him and he could ask for me if he wanted. He thanked me, adding that he would like me to visit him again. I closed the interview because I believed Mr. Stevens was tired. I realized that we had touched on something painful at the end and that he was avoiding it. But even so, I felt we had covered enough for the time being.

The worker is clear about her purpose in interviewing Mr. Stevens and consults his physician beforehand, learning the seriousness of his condition. Her observations of his appearance are careful and complete. He responds in a friendly fashion to her introduction of herself and perhaps feels a bond with her because her first name also is "Leslie."

Mr. Stevens originally denies having any problems, and presents himself as cooperating with hospital personnel, in contrast to the nurses' report of his lethargy. Rather than question his picture of himself, the worker decides to ask him about the most recent tests he has had; he claims not to know their purpose, but goes on to describe his discomfort.

The worker then encourages him to discuss his routine at home and he reveals a lonely life. Again, he voices no complaints and tells of the help given him by the wife of his superintendent. The worker might well have expressed more interest in what this woman does for him to ascertain the extent of her availability for helping him when he is discharged. Significant information about his passivity (or withdrawnness) is revealed when he tells how this woman and his niece took responsibility for getting him to the hospital when he became weak. The worker learns of the niece's concern and daily contacts with him during the hospitalization. One wonders why the worker responded that he seemed to have "a lot of people" looking after him, when, in fact, he has mentioned only these two. She too readily accepts "everyone knows me in the neighborhood"—perhaps because she is reluctant to acknowledge to herself, and point out to him, that he seems to lead a very lonely, isolated life. She does not, for instance, ask whom he sees or talks to when he goes out for lunch.

When the worker does refer to his feeling lonely, he becomes almost overwhelmed in talking about the death of his brother. He changes the subject to tell of his niece's invitation to stay with her and reveals his inability to be dependent on anyone when he is ill and unable to help them around the house as he used to be. The worker's assumption that the niece had offered him a permanent home, not just a temporary one, and the fact that she questions him again on his reasons for not living with his niece, may indicate her wish to find a happy solution for him in a home with his relatives. Despite his statements of realistic reasons such as his illness and the possibility of interfering in their lives, the worker has difficulty accepting his thinking. Recognizing his fatigue, the worker ends the interview, assuring him of her availability.

The worker's additional comments on the first interview reflect concern with his "sadness and loneliness." She was aware of "deeper feelings" that she did not know how to help him express and deal with. She had doubts about his ability to manage by himself on discharge and feared that he would not take the initiative to ask for help. She does not seem to be aware of the extent of his depression and the fact that he is still mourning for the brother who had been dead for a year. Despite these comments, the worker's sensitivity to her client's situation demonstrates that obtaining factual information does not preclude beginning to establish a helping relationship. The manner in which questions are asked, with sensitivity to the patient's feelings, conveys genuine concern and a wish to be of service.

10 "I want nice people to like me"

Needing and resisting help

Social workers frequently experience having persons referred to them for help who, for a multiplicity of reasons, do not want to discuss their problems and may, in fact, refuse to admit that any problems exist. This resistance may relate to fear of punitive action, as in referrals from courts for illegal or violent behavior, and in problems related to various forms of drug abuse. Other persons, because of emotionally deprived backgrounds and lifetimes of harsh, painful experiences, may be fearful of trusting other persons enough to confide in them. The following case from a medical setting illustrates how a worker, persistently demonstrating concern and friendly interest, enabled a young, disturbed woman with a history of drug abuse, promiscuous behavior, and several abortions to respond tentatively and express a wish to improve her life situation.

Joyce Owen, twenty-nine years old, had been admitted to the hospital on December 17, following an incomplete abortion (her fourth) which had become septic. A six-week program of antibiotics was begun for treatment of endocarditis. She had a history of drug abuse and was receiving methadone in the hospital clinic. The nurses found her to be a difficult patient, with outbursts of temper and screaming and one incident of smashing her intravenous-feeding bottle on the floor when she did not receive medication immediately. She asked to see a social worker to help her with a problem concerning her public assistance grant. A worker provided this service and another was assigned to offer help with her other evident problems.

Joyce Owen was an attractive white woman of medium height

and build. Her long, dark brown hair was clean and brushed. She used heavy makeup and wore blue jeans under her hospital gown and fashionable street shoes when she was not barefoot. She lived with her two-year-old son in an apartment and was supported by public assistance. Her parents lived nearby and she seemed to be close to her mother, who was taking care of her son during her hospitalization.

When the second social worker first saw her, on January 7, Joyce politely and firmly stated she did not want the help. She appreciated the help the first social worker had given her with her welfare problem; however, she wanted nothing further. She had no problems she wished to discuss. She just did not like to talk about herself to a social worker. The worker responded that she did not have to do anything that she did not want to; the worker would be available should she want to talk to someone and might come by occasionally to see how she was feeling. There were a few brief encounters later that day in the hospital hall, with an exchange of small talk.

The following day, Joyce invited the worker into her room "to watch TV." The worker said that she would like to come to talk with her, at which Joyce shrugged and said "Okay." Joyce talked mostly about her mother and her son. Her mother had returned to work and Joyce felt that her father could not care for her active child. The worker obtained information to enable Joyce's mother to arrange for a caretaker for her child.

Two days later, evidently in response to the worker's help in plans for her son's care, Joyce spoke with the worker again. She began with a torrent of talk about her past, including dropping out of high school, getting modeling jobs, and driving cars to Florida, when she took stimulants to stay awake so she could drive all night. She had started nurse's training, but was expelled when she had an abortion.

When she asked if the worker would reveal what they discussed, she laughed at the worker's assurance of confidentiality, saying: "I've heard that before." She tested the worker, asking if she would try to take her son away from her as another worker had tried.

The following excerpt continues the interview with the worker's response to Joyce's question:

I told her that from our conversations it sounded as if she loved her son very much. She did mention that he was hard to handle sometimes and that might be hard for her. I said that, if she realized she had problems with him, it might be good to talk with someone about them and to get further help. She said she believed me, that I did seem different from those other social workers; she usually didn't like social workers. I said that it sounded as if she had had some bad experiences with them. She said she really had, that I was different from the welfare social workers, too. I told her that here in the hospital, things were different. I wasn't there to determine her eligibility for assistance as welfare workers were or to judge her on those accounts. In the hospital, I saw a lot of different people with a lot of different needs. I was there to try to help with whatever those different needs might be. It might be to help straighten out some welfare problem she had, or it might be just to be there if someone needed someone else to talk to. She interjected that that's what she needed—someone to talk to. She didn't want any psychiatrist—she had been through that before. "They just sit there while you are pouring out your heart, and when you are saying your most personal things they look at their watch and say 'That's it.' And they never help you decide what to do." Oh, she knew they were not supposed to tell you what to do, they were supposed to help you come to your own decision. Well, that was all a bunch of bull—and you had to pay them for that? She wanted somebody like me to talk to. I told her that she had me—I would keep coming to see her.

Several mornings later, when I came to see her, Joyce wore hospital pants instead of her usual blue jeans. Her eye makeup was left over from the day before and was a little smeared under her eyes. I told her I was glad to see her, glad that she had decided to stay. (At our interview the previous evening, she had been very restless and had talked of checking out of the hospital.) She responded that she had felt better after I had left. They gave her some medication and she was going to try to last two more days, until her scheduled discharge date. While we were talking, hospital staff interrupted our conversation to change the linens. Joyce asked if we could go down to the solarium to talk, which we did.

Joyce began telling me about a patient on the floor who had been readmitted. She had become friendly with this patient, Sarah, a young black woman, but Sarah had started taking cigarettes from her and had tried to steal her lighter. Joyce felt that Sarah had taken advantage of her and talked at length about the details of her contacts with her. Then she asked me what I thought about her (Joyce), the way she talked, and our conversations. I asked her why she was asking me that. She said that she wanted to know if I liked her. I asked if it were important to her that people liked her? She went into a lengthy explanation about how important it was to her.

She told me that was all she wanted—for people to like her. She wanted "nice people" to like her: the hospital people, the nurses, and everybody. They were good people, and that class of people never liked her. Only low-class people liked her. She had done some really low things with her life and she just kept on. I said that it sounded as if she did not feel very good about herself. No, she replied, she didn't. Just as with Sarah, when Sarah came back and started talking with her again, Joyce started liking her again and giving her cigarettes. Then she stopped and asked herself, "Why am I doing this? This is the type of person I don't need for a friend, why do I keep talking with her? Am I so desperate for friends that I turn to people like her?" She stated she was that desperate; it had always been that way. When she was growing up, she had lived with what she considered to be low-class people—blacks and Spanish. She was always known as "the white girl" and she hated it. She wanted to be like them. She even tried talking with a Spanish accent. Then, when she was a teenager, she thought "all that low-class stuff" was really cool. She started dating a young man and thought it was great, because when she walked down the street people would look at her. But she didn't like that anymore. Sarah talked in "black street language." But those kinds of people were the only ones who would be friends with her. The low things she had done had really marked her. And people usually didn't change. She knew some addicts who had gone straight for up to five or six years, but then got strung out again. But she knew one guy who had really gone straight. He was her idol and she hung out at his place a lot. There were drugs around there because he still dealt some, but he never took any himself now. Her mother said that people couldn't change.

After a silence I said that I had seen people change. I told her to think about what she had said because she had said a lot. I said I was concerned over a lot of things she said, especially about her low feeling about herself. But it seemed that she had done some thinking and was aware of some things about herself. She said she thought she was now. She had just grown up too slowly. She figured that in her mind she might be about twenty years old now. She wished she could have been like this when she was twenty, then things might have been different. I told her that awareness was the first step to change, and she was aware of some things now and thought about them—that was healthy. She laughed and said she was glad I said there was something healthy up there (pointing to her head). She said she believed that, it probably was true. If she

could just be a good mother, it would wipe out everything she had
done in the past. I asked her to think about what we had talked
about and said I would come back to see her later.

In the above interview, the worker observes that Joyce is con-
forming to the usual hospital clothing but has ignored her old and
smeared makeup. The worker begins by expressing pleasure that
Joyce has decided to stay until her scheduled discharge date. Undoubtedly, this remark pleases Joyce, who responds that she had
"felt better" after their previous talk.

Joyce gives an account of another patient, and then leads into
trying to find out what the worker thinks of her, and continues to
express a need to be liked and accepted by "nice people." A beginning trust in the worker, who has shown concern for her despite
initial rebuffs, enables Joyce to reveal her lack of self-esteem, a
history of socially unacceptable behavior, and association with drug
addicts and pushers. She is relieved when the worker states her belief that some people can change; Joyce then expresses a wish to be
a good mother to her child as a way of wiping out her past
misbehavior.

Although Joyce opens up considerably in this interview, she
still keeps away from the subject of her own addiction. Aware of
the tenuous nature of their relationship, the worker does not, at any
time, initiate a discussion of her use of drugs. The worker had been
given a clue in a previous interview when a nurse came to give Joyce
medicine; Joyce had asked openly for the demerol but requested
that the nurse "hold off on the other" until the worker had left.

The worker records her impression that Joyce's initial appearance of being difficult and resistive to talking about herself to a
social worker is a facade. She sees Joyce as an immature, acting-out
child rather than an adult. Her rambling conversation seems to be
more characteristic of an adolescent than of a woman of twenty-
nine. The worker believes that Joyce is aware of having many problems, but Joyce is not certain that she has sufficient motivation to
change. Her addiction is a complicating factor. The worker has observed how anxious and restless Joyce becomes when the effects of
medication wear off. She is unable to tolerate delay in waiting for
medication.

It is the assessment of the client's need for affection and acceptance that influences the worker's comments, which in this interview
elicit a positive response from the client. The worker continues to
offer reassurance of her availability because the client has told her

of past experiences when she felt betrayed or let down by persons supposed to be helping her.

Although the worker realizes that she might not succeed, she hopes that Joyce would be able to maintain a contact with her after discharge. There was a brief farewell chat in which worker suggested Joyce come in to see her "just to talk" when she returned for her clinic appointments. Joyce did not indicate whether she would return to see the worker.

11 "What's going to happen to me now?"

Reassuring an abused child

The following two interviews from a child welfare agency show how interviewing may be used in preparing a child for placement. By means of her friendly interest and considerate explanations, the worker is able to change the child's hopeless anxiety in the face of a new and frightening situation into an acceptance of the change and even a certain expectancy that it will mean better days ahead. The child is freed from the feeling of being "pushed around" by having an opportunity to participate in preparations for the change.

Elaine, aged eleven, was referred to the intake division of a child welfare agency by the children's court for placement away from home. The court report stated that for about a year Elaine's stepfather had been engaged in sexual activities with her. Elaine, who had been born out of wedlock, had already gone through a series of unhealthy experiences because of her mother's promiscuity.

The court had given Elaine physical, psychological, and psychiatric examinations and found her healthy, intelligent, and friendly, but very upset about her experiences with her stepfather. She had been afraid to confide in her mother because her stepfather had threatened to kill her if she did. The psychiatrist recommended that Elaine be placed away from home, at least until her mother proved able to maintain a stable home.

In considering the type of care that would best meet Elaine's needs, the agency decided that a cottage-plan institution might be preferable at this time to a foster home. It was thought that it might be easier for her to adjust first in an institution where she would have an opportunity to relate herself to children and would have a wider choice in selecting an adult with whom she could identify. In planning Elaine's first placement in an institution, the agency hoped that after she had had an opportunity to readjust her first concepts of an adult world, she might then be placed in a foster home.

At the time of the court's referral to the agency, she had already spent three months at a children's detention home while the court's investigation was being made. Her mother had opposed placement but was finally forced to accept the authority of the court. Because of the delay in referral, the worker had only two days in which to prepare Elaine for placement. The following are her accounts of her two interviews with Elaine.

I first visited Elaine at the children's detention home. Before seeing Elaine, I arranged to take her out for an hour the following afternoon. I saw Elaine for about forty-five minutes. She was totally unprepared for my visit. She was completely bewildered by her present experience and asked, "What's going to happen to me now?" Elaine, a small, olive-skinned girl, thin and pathetic, with straight brown hair and a heart-shaped face, appeared quite terrified when she was brought down and introduced to me. She had tried unsuccessfully to improve her appearance by combing her hair in the latest fashion. The faded, ill-fitting clothes provided by the detention home did not improve her appearance. Her very large, dark eyes were sad, and several times tears welled up in her eyes and flowed down her cheeks. At times she seemed unable to speak because she would cry. In the midst of her tears she attempted to smile. Her lips would quiver. She would try to control herself, be unable to, cry, and then look up from under her lashes and try to brave a smile.

I introduced myself to Elaine, explaining that the court had asked our help in planning for her. I said I knew that she was unhappy in the detention home and bewildered about what was going to happen to her. Insofar as I could, in the short time we had, I would like to help her. Elaine's face lit up, and she tried very hard to smile, to show her appreciation, but it was difficult for her to smile without tears. Elaine and I spent some time discussing her present experience in the detention home. She told me that she had lost a good deal of weight since she had been there, both because she was unhappy and because she could not eat the food they served. She continued to talk about the detention home, expressing a great deal of resentment.

With a sad expression she said that she had been there longer than most of the children, and she thought it was a very long time. The monotony was relieved a little by visits from relatives. On the morning of the day I was there her mother, her sister, and her aunt had come to see her. With real feeling the child said, "My mother wants to take me home." She cried in a heartbreaking fashion. I said I was sure that her mother wanted to take her home but that perhaps it was not possible for her to go home yet. Her mother would first make a real home for her, and then she would go to live with her mother. Elaine continued to cry and to say that she wanted to go home with her mother, that she did not want to go anywhere else. With a sigh, the child said that she knew she really could not go home yet. The judge had talked to her, and he had explained to her that it was best for her to live somewhere else. In front of the judge her mother had said that she would try to make a good home for Elaine. Elaine said she had accepted the fact that she was going to be sent someplace. She was sure her mother would do everything to make it possible to take her home in the very near future; until that time, however, some other plan had to be made for her. She did not know what that plan was, but she felt sure that I could tell her.

Did my visit mean that I could get her out of the detention home? I said that was what I wanted to do and why I had come to see her, to talk to her about what was going to happen to her. Elaine said that strange things had been happening to her. Until the past few months she had not known about courts and judges and "horrible places" like the detention home. I said that these were unusual experiences for a child and painful ones. Elaine cried bitterly. She was so eager to get out of the home. She had not even been out of the building for the past three months. I said I had made arrangements to take her out for a walk the following day. We would spend an hour together, and she could plan the hour in whatever way she liked. At this point Elaine gave me a really genuine smile. I commented on it, saying that I had not been sure she knew how to smile; that when she smiled her face lit up, she was so pretty. Elaine managed a laugh at that and said she would spend the rest of her waking hours planning for our time the next day. I said that besides taking her out, I wanted to talk with her about some other matters.

Her change in residence would come about in two days. I thought she might like to know something about the place to which she was going. Elaine shyly smiled and said that she would. I told her about the physical setup; the name, which she thought was very nice; the sewing class; the school; the activities in the institution; and so on. Elaine said that she could crochet and that she was making a washcloth. She was interested in the sewing class. She was also interested in the toys. Elaine said she could ride a bicycle and could skate. She liked to cook, and the idea of helping in the cottages appealed to her. She told me some of the things she could cook and was pleased that she could make rather fancy dishes. She was interested in the library at the institution and said that she had previously belonged to a library. She asked about the ages of the children there, about the cottage mothers, and so on.

I said that the whole idea of this institution must be very new to Elaine. Since I was sure she could not at that time think of all the questions she would like to ask, I would leave her a pencil and paper, and she could write down all the questions that came to her mind. When I saw her the following day, we could go over the list of questions. Elaine seemed very pleased with this arrangement—more pleased, I thought, because she was keeping something tangible to remind her that I was real than because she would be able to ask questions. (This thought was confirmed the next day. Although Elaine had left the paper and pencil upstairs, she remembered all the questions she wanted to ask me.) Elaine squeezed my hand when I left her and became very cheerful when she said she would be dressed and ready to go out for a walk when I came the following day.

The following day I met Elaine at the detention home. She was dressed in her own clothes and ready to go out. When I first came, she was smiling broadly and ran to meet me. Although her clothes were torn and patched, her appearance was dignified. She took my hand immediately and held it tightly throughout the hour we spent together.

Elaine had planned the hour in this way: She first wanted to walk in the sunshine; then she wanted to go to a department store and look at toys. It was interesting to watch Elaine change from a dignified, stiff little girl into a prancing, happy child. She fairly danced after she got used to me and the freedom and the fresh air. When she was ready, we went to the department store she had selected and took the elevator up to the toy department. When we had entered the store, Elaine had looked at me coyly and said that she would like to start with the boys' side first. She was interested in most of the boys' toys, particularly in an electric train. With a cute smile and a flirtatious glance she said, "In my neighborhood I'm known as quite a tomboy." When we finished the boys' side and went to the girls' side, Elaine was much less interested. Occasionally *she would comment on a doll, saying that she had one like it or her sister had one like it. On the whole, she was not interested in the girls' toys. On the way out of the store we stopped at a fountain to get a drink. Elaine had a pineapple soda with chocolate ice cream, which she drank with a good deal of gusto.*

During the hour we were able to talk a little about the institution. Occasionally, she would see a toy and ask whether they had one like it there. I told Elaine the details of what would be happening to her the following day in court. I explained that I would not be there because I had to be at the institution on that day. Since I would be at the institution, I would, however, have an opportunity to tell them about her so that they would be expecting her when she came. I gave her a brief description of the people she would meet when she first got there.

When we got back to the detention home, Elaine said that the hour had passed all too fast. When I got ready to leave, she thanked me and looked up at me with a sort of questioning look. I leaned over and she put both arms around my neck and kissed me. She then turned her face away and giggled. I gave her a reassuring smile and squeezed her hand; then she went upstairs with the matron.

Elaine comes to life for us in the interviewer's vivid portrayal. The description reveals a discerning observation of a child. In all adequate interviewing, even as the external greetings are taking place, internal mental notes are being made. The worker's first activity is always guided by early observations. Here the worker immediately sees a frightened, bewildered child. As a result, she takes the initiative, for she realizes that a child precipitated into such a bewildering situation would feel lost, anxious, and insecure in the face of an unknown future. Having been plunged into an unfamiliar detention home, not knowing from day to day what may happen to her, Elaine feels completely at the mercy of grown-ups. She is filled with a sense of futility and helplessness in the face of their overpowering strength and authority.

In addition to realizing how the girl feels, the worker knows that she must take the initiative because Elaine has not asked for an interview and has no idea why she is being sought out. The worker, therefore, attempts to put the child at ease by telling her at once why she has come, thus freeing her as much as possible from her natural fear of another new and perhaps calamitous experience. The worker indicates that she wants to be Elaine's friend, something a child can understand. She lets Elaine know also that she understands how Elaine feels about the detention home, as well as her feelings of uncertainty about what will happen to her.

One important aspect of the first interview consists in allowing the child to express—what she had been unable to mention with others—her dislike of the detention home and her unhappiness there. Another is the worker's attempt to visualize as simply and concretely as possible for Elaine what she can expect in the new home to which she will be going. As concrete evidence to the child of her friendliness, she arranges to take her out of the home for an hour and promises to let Elaine choose how they will spend that time. If Elaine had not been given any opportunity to talk against the detention home, she might have had to bottle up her resentment. By expressing herself, she "gets it off her chest." Further, the very fact of the worker's sympathetic understanding makes it possible for Elaine to regard her many recent troubles as less intolerably unjust.

Although the worker takes the initiative in this interview, it is initiative of a quite different sort from that taken by the court in placing the child in the detention home with a vague explanation. The initiative of the worker stimulates Elaine to participate in the plans being made. It is valuable for even a young child to have some feeling that he has a share in important decisions about his own future. It may not be possible to allow Elaine to choose, for instance, whether she will remain with her mother or live away from home, whether she will live in an institution or a foster home, or to choose the institution or foster home in which she will live. In these areas the agency must take the responsibility for her protection and use its better judgment. Elaine would have no basis on which to make such choices. We cannot make a free choice unless we know what the alternatives are. In the face of these necessary limitations, the worker arranges for an hour's walk during which Elaine will be completely free to determine what they will do. An ingenious worker will always find some areas in which she can leave decisions to her client, stimulating him to initiative and independent choice and giving him the feeling that he still has some control of the situation.

Here, the worker also does what she can to let Elaine participate as much as possible in the plans being made for her. She is encouraged to talk about them whenever she has enough interest and knowledge to do so. For instance, the worker offers to answer any questions about the new home that come to Elaine's mind, but she does not volunteer information beyond Elaine's present interest or ken.

Elaine might have asked, "Will they want a little girl like me who has been bad?" In that case the worker might have talked with her further about her experiences with her stepfather, but because Elaine did not bring these experiences up, the worker did not push her. Undoubtedly Elaine will need to talk with someone about the experiences she has had, but if the worker had at such an early point indicated that she wanted Elaine to talk about them, Elaine might well have felt that it was too soon to discuss such matters with a stranger.

The worker implies by her attitude that she understands and wants to help, and that there will be others in the new home who will help. Her acceptance of the child's resentment against the detention home gives Elaine some security by showing her that there are understanding people in the world with whom one can talk. The worker's sensitive observation of the child's slightest expression is indicated in her recognition of Elaine's desire to kiss her. The worker's natural, unembarrassed response is an appropriate one to a frightened, friendless child.

The concrete purpose of these interviews was to prepare Elaine to be emotionally ready to accept a new home so that she could go into it with some feeling of security. Such preparation was especially important here because Elaine's many unfortunate experiences would otherwise have led her to expect the worst from another sudden change thrust upon her. This attitude would, in turn, have jeopardized the success of her placement. The danger was lessened by the interviewer's leading Elaine to look forward with hope to going to her new home.

12 "Nobody would really want to help me"

Counseling in a union setting

The provision of social services as one of an industry's employee benefit programs or as one of a labor union's membership benefits has been growing at a rapid pace within the past decade. Viewed from the perspective of industrial management, such a program contributes to employee efficiency and, therefore, maximizes company profits. To the union, a personal counseling service is an important membership benefit increasingly in demand. Regardless of sponsorship, such counseling programs are based on a recognition of the psychological and emotional significance of work for the maintenance of mental health and individual self-esteem.

Experience has shown that for many workers today, the work place and the job itself function as more of a support system than does the family. Problems encountered at the work place as well as problems that interfere with an individual's job performance can seriously endanger one's sense of security and satisfaction with one's life. Presented below are two interviews with a woman employee experiencing severe anxiety in relation to her job. They were drawn from the files of a labor union's personal counseling service.

The labor union to which Mrs. Edith Clark belongs has a policy of referring members who have to leave their jobs because of disability to the Personal Service Unit of its health plan for counseling service and any help in planning that they may need. Mrs. Clark's name was given to the Personal Service Unit by the Disability Unit with a notation that she had had a heart attack. When the Personal Service worker telephoned her (Mrs. Clark had not contacted the unit herself), he learned that she had developed a thyroid condition whose symptoms initially had confused the doctors. By the time

Mrs. Clark came to the arranged appointment, she had returned to work and wanted to talk to the counselor about problems she was having on the job. What follows is the counselor's recording of two of his interviews and a summary of other contacts, as well as commentary about the interviewing process.

During our telephone contact before her first interview, Mrs. Clark said that she had started working in a new position just before she had had to go out on disability, thinking she was having problems with her heart. She had been promoted to her first supervisory position. The department in which she worked was difficult, and she had requested a transfer to an easier one. She had presented a letter from her doctor stating that although she could return to work, he recommended that she be given a less stressful job. Her employer did not want to transfer her, and she did not know why he refused. She wanted to come to see me because she was feeling overwhelmed. She did not know whether she would be able to handle her job situation. My immediate concern was to help her through the crisis she was experiencing, both through counseling and by involving the union representative in her situation.

Our first interview got off to a poor start. I was running late with my appointments that day and Mrs. Clark had to wait fifteen minutes. When we were seated in my cubicle, I apologized for keeping her waiting. She was visibly upset and had tears in her eyes. She said that she felt I didn't really care either. I assured her I could not help the delay, and that I rarely kept anyone waiting. I suggested that the wait had touched off how she had already been feeling inside. When she agreed to that, I asked her to tell me about what was going on.

Mrs. Clark immediately began to tell me what she had been going through. At work, she continually felt that she was going to cry. She did not feel that she knew what she was doing or that she was in control of the situation. She was especially having a hard time with her main boss. She did not feel that anyone there was really giving her support. I expressed my concern and sympathy for what she had been going through and asked if she had turned to the union for direct help with her job.

Mrs. Clark replied that she had not contacted the union at all; she did not believe that anyone would really want to help her. I assured her that the union would be interested in helping her, and, just as importantly, it was her right as a member of the union to ask for help. She said she would be willing to try. I told her that I would speak to the union representative for her and asked her if she would be willing to sign a release of information form. I explained that it would allow me to share information with the representative. She agreed to sign it, adding that she just hoped it would be of some help.

I then asked Mrs. Clark some questions concerning her physical condition. She showed me the letter from her doctor stating that she should not return to a stressful situation. When I asked her how she was feeling, she replied that she had a tightness in her chest, which she thought was caused by anxiety. I told her that I was concerned about her physical condition and would speak to the union representative right away. I also suggested she think about going on disability again, if her physical condition seemed to be getting worse. I also said that I thought we would be able to help her, both through counseling and through the union's intervention.

I could see that she was feeling a bit calmer. When I asked her if this was so, she acknowledged that just the thought that someone was going to try to help her was making her a little less anxious. Because I was very worried about her physical condition and the stress she was feeling on the job, I said I would like to show her a simple breathing exercise she could use during the day to help her relax when she was feeling overwhelmed. She was interested in this idea. She said that she liked getting suggestions of techniques to help her. I believe my teaching her this technique made her feel less helpless. Also, it showed me she could make good use of such aids in handling her job situation. I showed her how to do the exercise and recommended she use it as often as she needed. I also told her that if it didn't work I had many other ideas. I also suggested that she call me any time she felt too much pressure. She thanked me for making that offer and then started to cry. I let her know that I understood how hard it is when one feels alone in trouble, and that I was happy to be here helping her with it now.

Knowing she was married, I asked her what role her family played in her situation. She remarked that although her husband was supportive, she did not feel that he was able to give her the kind of help she needed. She thought that he was having a hard time dealing with how upset she was. A number of very difficult situations had recently happened in her personal life. One was the death of her mother-in-law. During her mother-in-law's last illness, Mrs. Clark had taken a major role in looking after her. The family doctor had felt that Mr. Clark could not handle the situation. Then, more recently, Mrs. Clark's son by her first husband began failing in school and associating with a group of boys who seemed always to be in trouble. In this situation, also, her husband had not been able to deal with what was happening and she had tried to handle the problem by herself.

We spent a few minutes discussing how she felt about taking all these responsibilities on herself. She was aware that it was a basic problem of hers and thought it was part of the reason she was having a problem on the job. She was supposed to be a supervisor, but it was difficult for her to tell anyone else what to do. She usually found it easier to do things herself. When I asked her how it usually went when she tried to supervise, she said that her words often came out as too sharp or with anger. She didn't know why. I suggested that a combination of feeling overwhelmed and not really believing that people would listen to her might cause her to express herself in anger. She said she was not sure. I suggested she make a note of each time she found herself in that kind of situation and we would discuss it.

I also told Mrs. Clark that we would work together on strategies for handling her work and techniques for dealing with her superiors at work and also those people working under her. I told her that I sensed she was not able to recognize the effect her physical condition was having on her nerves and that probably in a short time some of the exhaustion and strain she was feeling would lessen. I also stressed that it was a temporary situation, one that would pass, and that she should try to take one day at a time. I then told her our time was up. She said she was feeling better, that I had helped her to feel she could do it. It was so nice to know someone was going to be helping her. I reminded her to call me if she needed to. I also said I would contact her as soon as I had some idea from the union representative where things stood. We made an appointment for the following week. I planned to see her in the early evening because Mrs. Clark did not have time off from work coming to her.

My basic concern during this first interview was to leave Mrs. Clark with the feeling that I really thought I would be able to help her. I also wanted to convey that there might be something concrete that could be done by the union. I think these comments helped to quiet some of her anxiety.

This interview illustrates the counselor's success in establishing a working relationship with a woman who is seemingly convinced that no one can help her, and then shifting her attitude from one of pessimism to one of hopefulness. The content of the interview is the problem as defined by the client herself, her personal anxieties in relation to her job and the strains of her new work role as supervisor. The counselor opens the interview by apologizing for his tardiness. His taking responsibility for the added pressure he has placed on Mrs. Clark helps to establish his trustworthiness, which should encourage Mrs. Clark to view him as a person who will, indeed, be able to give her assistance in dealing with her anxieties. He then skillfully helps Mrs. Clark acknowledge that she is reacting in part to the internal concerns she has brought with her, and he suggests that they talk further about these concerns.

A substantial portion of the interview is the counselor's repeated reassurance that Mrs. Clark will receive help both from him and from the union and his assertion that she has a right to ask for such help. Although he offers a greater amount of reassurance than is customarily warranted, his responses to Mrs. Clark's obvious intense feeling of being alone, rejected, and unhelped with her problems are both ego-supportive and therapeutic. Moreover, he offers to take direct action (speaking to the union representative) on her behalf. One senses that the counselor is correct in his judgment that Mrs. Clark requires concrete evidence of his helpfulness to counteract her pessimistic attitude. That he is correct in his assessment of Mrs. Clark's neediness is evidenced by her becoming calmer and less anxious as the interview progresses.

It is possible that the counselor, out of lack of experience, misses the probable significance of the threat posed to Mrs. Clark by her promotion to a supervisory position. She herself states that she thought that the "tightness in her chest" is "caused by anxiety." The counselor's response is to again express his concern about her physical condition. It is conceivable that her anxiety about her new job responsibilities actually precipitated her physical symptoms, and the counselor might have helped her more had he opened up this area for discussion.

Another feature of this interview is the counselor's decision to teach Mrs. Clark a relaxation exercise. Because work stress and anxiety are among her chief problems, and the ones for which she is seeking counseling help, his decision to employ this device is probably appropriate. Mrs. Clark's positive response so indicates.

In the counselor's exploration of Mrs. Clark's life and relationships outside the work setting, he gathers important information about her tendency to assume burdens and do things herself—a ten-

dency she, too, sees as related to some of her pressures on the job.
He offers a direct interpretation of the cause of her inability to be
comfortable in her new supervisory role and suggests that they examine this area in more detail in future contacts. One has the feeling that Mrs. Clark comes to believe that she would get the help she
needed.

Following this interview, the counselor talked several times
with the union representative to enlist his help in obtaining Mrs.
Clark's transfer to a less stressful office, which was the doctor's
recommendation. The union representative expressed his opinion
that Mrs. Clark was, indeed, in a difficult work environment and
that her current superior might force her to again be placed on disability status if she complained about the work pressures. Although
the union representative at first feared that arranging a transfer
would be difficult, Mrs. Clark did eventually receive a transfer to a
quieter, less stressful location. When she had first learned of this
possibility she voiced some reluctance to move lest it look as if she
were "giving up," and she called the counselor to discuss it. The
interview below was held three weeks after her move to the new
office.

*Mrs. Clark came into the interviewing cubicle with a smile. She
repeated what she had told me in a recent phone call, that things
had been going well. (She felt it had helped her a lot to be able to
phone me when she needed to, although she had done it rarely.)
We discussed what had been happening on the new job. She had
been using a technique we had discussed of writing down what she
planned to say and then studying it. She found that this rehearsal
technique made it much easier for her to talk. She had been able to
tell her supervisor the things she had wanted to. She also felt he had
been very nice to her, he really wanted things to go well. On the
previous job, she had felt that she had not been properly trained or
prepared. This time, she was able to make clear what her needs
were. Also, she had decided against letting her new supervisor
know what a hard time she had had on the other job. She thought it
was wise not to give him all that information. I agreed, saying, "If
you were to tell him what a hard time you had, then he might interpret any problems you have now as meaning you're finding things
too difficult."*

*Mrs. Clark then discussed how things had gone with the two
persons working under her. Here also she had written down what*

she planned to say. She also remembered some things we had re-hearsed last week and which she had been able to use. Particularly helpful for her was trying to think of how she would want to be spoken to and what would make her respond positively. Then she would try to do the same with other people.

I congratulated Mrs. Clark on handling things so well. She im-mediately let me know that things were not all that good. She was still having a very hard time doing the job. She still found herself wanting to cry at times. I said that I realized everything was not changed by a new situation. However, I did think it was important for her to take note of how well she had been doing and the im-provements she had made since we had started to work together. She said that that was true. She was aware of how much better things were. She then thanked me for the help I had given her. I told her how happy I was to have been of help to her.

I asked her to tell me about the current situation. We discussed the problems involved in being on a new job and the natural amount of anxiety that it created. I commented that, when looked at in relation to everything that had happened before, it was not surprising that she was having a hard time. I said I thought that as the job became routine, she would find it easier. I also said that I thought the more she believed that she could find successful ways to handle situations, the more comfortable she would be in her role of supervisor. She said she hoped so.

Mrs. Clark then asked me if I thought that she could apply what she learned here to the rest of her life. I asked her to be more specific. She said that she felt as if she needed to learn to assert herself more in her private life also. She was tired of taking every-thing on herself. I replied that it was very likely that what she had learned in handling this situation she would be able to apply to other things in her life. I then suggested that she could discuss any situations she wanted to with me; it didn't have to be just about work.

The fact that Mrs. Clark was bringing up her personal life was an indication that she was no longer in the same state of anxiety that had brought her to see me. Also, it was possible that I had gained her trust to a greater degree and she now wanted to talk about other areas besides work.

Mrs. Clark proceeded to share a problem that had been on her mind; whether her second husband was an alcoholic. Her first hus-band had been an alcoholic, and this fact had been hard for her to face. She had been able to deal with it only after she had gone to

Al-Anon and finally into therapy. She had found that therapy had been very helpful, which is why she had positive feelings about coming here for help. She really liked Al-Anon and was still an active member. That was one of the reasons she was having a hard time admitting that she might have gotten into the same situation again.

Mrs. Clark then said that her father had been an alcoholic. She was concerned that she was not going to be able to really change her life. We discussed how she saw herself and what she thought people would think of her if she told them what she had told me. We only scratched the surface of this matter and of her relationship with her husband. But I felt that we had made a bridge that would allow her to bring all of her concerns to counseling. We made an appointment for next week.

Apparently, Mrs. Clark's transfer to a new work setting was a good move. In this interview she makes quite a different impression from that made by her previous demeanor. Her mood is elevated, and it is clear that she has made genuine progress. Things are going much better for her at work. Moreover, her statement that she is "tired of taking everything on herself," is indicative of a stronger ego and greater ability to assert herself than she possessed when she first sought help.

On the other hand, Mrs. Clark reveals her need not to lose the counselor's interest and support when she insists that her problems are not completely solved. She seemed to be telling the counselor that she needs further contact with him when she proudly reports that she has been using the relaxation and rehearsal techniques he has taught her—verification that a firm treatment relationship has been established. When Mrs. Clark returns to her earlier skepticism about her ability to handle her job stresses, the counselor suggests that she acknowledge the progress she has made and look forward to making even more progress in the future.

This interview also demonstrates that the counselor has kept as the main focus of treatment the core problem Mrs. Clark brought to the Personal Service Unit—her work adjustment. Success in this area is evident. It is also significant that Mrs. Clark raises a question about applying what she has learned in relation to handling her work stress to other areas of her life. The counselor shows his interviewing skill when he avoids answering Mrs. Clark's question directly and asks her to be specific about what she has in mind. This question elicits from Mrs. Clark information about her marital concerns and her wish for further help in this area. It is likely that the counselor's future work with Mrs. Clark will be less clearly focused on the job situation, although a client's work adjustment remains a chief responsibility of the union counseling service.

13 "We don't want to be a burden"

Assessing needs of elderly parents

The interview in this chapter illustrates the skills required to establish a helping relationship with elderly persons, particularly those who cling tenaciously to their diminishing independence. The clients in this instance, Mr. and Mrs. Parsons, are typical of a growing number of aging parents who live by themselves but whose adult children feel a sense of responsibility for them. Family service agencies, such as the one from whose files this interview was drawn, have been expanding their services to aged individuals. Frequently, as in this situation, the request for service is not made by the aging individual himself but by a concerned relative or close friend. Such a person may also benefit from counseling to learn how to be of the greatest help to the aging person or to handle feelings of guilt or excessive responsibility, feelings that are not warranted.

The initial request for service for Charles and Gertrude Parsons, a married couple in their mid-seventies, was made by their forty-eight-year-old son, Alfred, who telephoned the family service agency to ask for an evaluation of his aged parents' needs. He mentioned having an unmarried sister, Laura, who is also concerned about Mr. and Mrs. Parsons. An assistant professor of chemistry at an out-of-state college, she keeps in touch with her parents regularly by telephone. Alfred Parsons owns a small insurance company and lives in the suburbs. In requesting service for his parents, who live in an old neighborhood in the city, he said that lately his mother has been telling him and his sister that maintaining the apartment is too much for her and that perhaps she and their father need to live somewhere else—possibly in a home for the aged. This thinking represents a change, inasmuch as Mrs. Parsons has always refused help in the house. Both parents have physical problems and Alfred and Laura are glad that Mr. and Mrs. Parsons are ready to consider alternatives. He said that his mother knows he has called the agency and a home visit can be arranged directly with her. He described her as "the decision maker" in the household.

When the worker telephoned to arrange the time of the home visit, Mrs. Parsons willingly agreed to an interview but made it clear that she was very independent in spite of failing health. She was meticulous in giving the worker directions for finding the apartment located in a large building reserved for the elderly. The worker's recording of the interview follows:

I arrived a few minutes early but Mrs. Parsons greeted me at the door as I stepped from the elevator. She was wearing a colorful, flowered robe. She looked at me with curiosity from behind the thick glasses she wears because of cataracts and remarked, "Oh, you look younger than I imagined!" She smiles warmly and readily. Mr. Parsons was seated when I entered and immediately grasped my hand in welcome. They indicated that I should sit anywhere I liked and I selected a chair. Mrs. Parsons sat on a couch to my left and Mr. Parsons sat across the room. As we started talking, it was difficult for me to maintain eye contact with both of them—something Mr. Parsons sensed and he moved next to his wife.

They both seemed a bit ill at ease. When I asked them why their son felt it necessary to call the agency at this time and what was the precipitating factor, Mrs. Parsons jumped in to answer. She explained that her son has always been concerned about their health and worries about them a lot. He has three children, a daughter in college and two sons, aged thirteen and nine years. Mrs. Parsons thinks that their son has all he can handle taking care of his own family. Laura is also concerned about her parents but is too far away to see them as often as she and they would like. Mrs. Parsons suffers from diabetes; Mr. Parsons had influenza this past year as well as a prostate operation. Mr. Parsons looked quite well today but I noticed that Mrs. Parsons moves slowly. She said that their children worry too much about them.

Until this point I was listening to Mrs. Parsons explain about her and her husband, and I sympathized that it must have been difficult for them when Mr. Parsons was in the hospital for his surgery. I asked them to tell me how they like their apartment, how they manage with all of the chores, and so on. A housekeeper comes in once a week and is paid to do the laundry and all of the cleaning. (The apartment is of manageable size; there is a bath-

*room, a nice-sized living room, a small modern kitchen, and a spa-
cious bedroom.) They send out for all their groceries when they
need them and pay an extra $1.25 to have them delivered. I men-
tioned home-delivered meals, which they know about, but Mrs. Parsons was quick to tell me that she likes to do the cooking. They eat
lightly but very nutritiously.*

*I asked them in detail about their finances after Mrs. Parsons
said they are independent financially. They have savings in the bank
and they collect interest on that every three months, as well as receiving their Social Security checks. Their rent is $160 monthly. I
asked them how they feel about their apartment. Mrs. Parsons said
that they had been in this building for eight years and they liked it
very much. "It is quiet and it is spotlessly clean." She talked about
all the hustle and bustle when they visit their son's family and said
they can't fall asleep there; they like being in their own beds. They
consider their apartment affordable, and they do not want to dig
into their savings unless they absolutely have to. We totaled up all
their expenses against their income, and they do seem to be handling their expenditures without too much strain.*

In this interview the worker adheres closely to the purpose for
which the home visit was made. To assess what Mr. and Mrs. Parsons need and whether some alternative living arrangements should
be considered, she inquires about their health and asks them to tell
her in detail the practical arrangements they have made for household management. The worker further records that she asked about
their finances "*after* Mrs. Parsons said they are independent financially." Apparently, the worker senses that this couple might be
reluctant to talk about their financial status and she is respectful of
their feelings. Such reluctance to discuss money matters is not un-
common among the elderly, and the worker shows her sensitivity in
her handling of this discussion.

*I asked them about the other living arrangements that their son
and daughter have suggested. First, their son found an apartment
for them costing $70 more a month than they are paying now and
which was closer to where he lives. Although their children would
have paid the difference, it was evident that they do not want the
children to assist them. With great determination in her voice, Mrs.
Parsons said, "We don't want to be a burden. And we don't want
our children to worry about us." They think their son has as much
responsibility as he can handle and their daughter's salary is only
enough to cover her expenses. Mrs. Parsons said that the $35 each*

of the children would contribute if they rented the other apartment would be more difficult for them than if the Parsons themselves had to part with it. It is also important to them to be able to buy gifts for their grandchildren. If they moved to a place that was more expensive, they would not have money for the little luxuries. They are afraid to be left with nothing, but they also know they would never be put out on the street.

Mr. and Mrs. Parsons seemed to be very realistic about their situation. They said that they have made a life for themselves, that "Sure, it's a little lonesome at times," but they have their own way of doing things, and that as long as they are here they want to do what they can without having to depend on anyone. I said, "You seem to have things under control and apparently have been taking good care of each other." Mrs. Parsons linked her arm in her husband's and it was really touching to see that they take a lot of pride in how they are balancing their budget, relying on each other, and following their doctors' orders. They spoke of the closeness between them and their children and grandchildren. It was evident that they do not feel neglected or unloved. They also commented on how their daughter-in-law phones them every day and they are very fond of her.

To bring the interview to a close, I said, "I do want to call your son and let him know that I saw you both. Maybe he will want to address some of his own concerns, too. It sounds as if everyone in your family is worried about each other!" They thanked me very much for coming and I said that it was a pleasure to meet them both. They seemed willing to pay whatever fee I asked but I suggested only $3.00, explaining that it was the agency's policy to ask for payment on a sliding scale. They said they could pay $5.00 but I told them $3.00 was enough.

If I have assessed this situation correctly, Mr. and Mrs. Parsons should remain in their current apartment unless one of them becomes disabled. I plan to call Alfred Parsons to let him know of my assessment and to tell him I shall be glad to talk with him about any concerns he may have. I think it probable that he is finding it hard to see his parents deteriorating. He and his wife would probably find it easier if his parents lived nearer to them so they could step in more quickly should an emergency arise.

A few days later, I talked with Alfred Parsons. He said, "I want to thank you very much. I don't know what you did, but you seem to have worked miracles with my parents. My mother had been very depressed and that is why I called the agency in the first place. She was the one who mentioned a home for the aged." He

*added that I seemed to have given his parents positive reinforce-
ment of their ideas about maintaining their independence. I commented to him that like many fearful, aged persons, his parents
seemed to vacillate between expressions of adequacy and feelings of
helplessness. He said he is relieved to see his mother in a more
optimistic mood but he still worries a great deal about them, as does
his wife. He asked if I could visit them again if something happened
that they needed advice and help. I assured him of my availability
and continued interest. He seemed reluctant to end the conversation, again repeating his appreciation. I said I knew how concerned he, his wife, and his sister were about his parents and asked
if he would like to talk with me further about their concerns. He
accepted the suggestion eagerly and we made an appointment for
him and his wife for the following week.*

Possibly the outstanding feature of this interview is the clients'
need and determination to maintain their independence. It was especially important for the worker to respect this need in light of the
danger that the adult children, out of their genuine concern, might
infringe on their parents' right to make their own decisions. The
worker herself risked infantilizing this couple when she suggested a
smaller fee for service than they were willing to pay. Their strong
feelings of wanting to maintain their dignity and self-respect were
expressed in their insistence that they could pay the higher amount.
It might have been more satisfying to them if the worker had hon-
ored their wish in this respect.

The Parsons case also illustrates an increasingly frequent phenomenon as the average life span of both men and women length-
ens: the need for adult children to take part in planning for the care
of their aged parents. Middle-aged couples who are still supporting
adolescent children may be called upon to assume some responsibility for their parents as well. Although Mr. and Mrs. Parsons
were fortunate in not having to rely upon their son and daughter,
the worker recognized the son's legitimate concern and offered
counseling help to him and his wife, which he clearly welcomed.

14 "Will I be labeled as a child abuser in the computers?"

Preventing possible child abuse

This chapter presents the interviewing process with persons possibly involved in family violence—specifically, child abuse. In the past few years, increasing pressure has been placed on hospitals, social agencies, physicians, school personnel, and others to report instances of suspected child abuse to public child protection agencies. In some states, there are laws requiring such reporting. When the child protection worker's investigation reveals that abuse has in fact occurred and that a family member is the abuser, referral is often made to a family service or child welfare agency for counseling. In these situations the abusive parent is likely to have been coerced into counseling and has not voluntarily sought help with his or her abusive behavior. The counselor's first task must be to engage the abusing parent in treatment.

The interview that follows records the caseworker's first contact with the family. Marilyn Mosher, twenty-eight years of age, her two sons, ten-year-old Jeff and eight-year-old Billy, and Mrs. Mosher's thirty-five-year-old companion, Tim Breslin, with whom they lived, had been referred to the family service agency by the child protective service worker. The protective service worker had been called by the principal at the school the boys attended. She had requested an investigation because both boys had come to school and complained about bruises on their buttocks. After seeing the boys' injuries, the protective service worker telephoned Mrs. Mosher, who in turn called Mr. Breslin and they went to the school together. The worker talked with them and asked them to take the boys to the protective service pediatrician for an examination. The doctor found that the injuries were not serious. Both Mrs. Mosher and Mr. Breslin acknowledged that he had spanked the boys because they had hidden their report cards and lied about their poor grades. It was the protective service worker's impression that this was an isolated incident and that the adults might profit from counseling in relation to learning how to deal with the boys and their behavior. The couple readily accepted the referral.

The family was on time for an early morning appointment. After introducing myself, I spoke to the children first, asking their names and ages. I then asked if they knew what this meeting was about. They both shook their heads. I explained that I was a social worker trained to help families that are having problems, adding, "Now can you figure out what this is about?" Billy said, "Yes, we hid our report cards." I turned to Jeff and asked if they had done this together. He replied, "Yes. We were scared that we wouldn't be able to go camping."

I asked Mrs. Mosher and Mr. Breslin if camping was an important family activity. Mr. Breslin replied that they had gone camping only once, over a year ago. When I asked the boys if they had enjoyed it, their faces—Billy's especially—lit up and they told me what they had done on the camping trip. There was laughter, and everyone interacted, telling about the trip.

I then asked, "What happened after you hid the report cards?" Billy replied, "We got a whipping." (When I addressed questions to both boys, Billy would be the spokesman. Jeff only responded when addressed individually.) "Then what?" I asked. Billy replied, "We went to school and the teachers saw our bruises." "Oh," I said, "I bet you won't hide your report cards again!" Nervous laughter from everyone followed. I then turned to the adults asking how the boys have been doing since then. Their mother replied, "They lie a lot." I asked for an example and Mr. Breslin explained that they were not allowed to go swimming in the apartment complex pool without an adult. While he is sleeping they sneak out, but they deny it when he confronts them. When I asked what other concerns they have about the children, Mr. Breslin spoke about their poor academic performance. I asked their mother what their grades had been, and she said they were mostly Ds and Fs. I asked if these were usually the grades or if they were a recent occurrence, and she replied that the boys had always done poorly in school. According to Mr. Breslin, they are doing somewhat better lately. He and their mother have been working with the boys some, but he has no faith in the schools. When I wondered aloud if that had something to do with the way the school handled the boys' bruises, he replied that they had gone to the school and asked for help with the boys, but they had not gotten any help, only the mess that followed the poor report cards. I said that the school had a legal responsibility to report the bruises, yet I let him know that I agreed with him that the public schools left much to be desired.

I then asked Mr. Breslin how long he had known this family. He replied, "About a year." I asked Mrs. Mosher how she had met him. They met at a singles dance. The next day she had taken the children to a singles club picnic, and, by plan, had met him there. A few weeks later, she and the children moved into his apartment. I turned to the boys and asked, "Where is your natural father?" "With another lady," said Billy, who began to cry and said, "I want to see him." I asked when he had last seen him and he replied that it was a couple of years ago. Mr. Breslin then said to Mrs. Mosher, "Maybe you should ask her about this." She frowned and looked uncomfortable. I asked her where the boys' father was, and she said that he was here in the city but that they have not seen him in a long time. When I asked whether Billy often cried about his father, his mother replied, "Never." Mr. Breslin added, "This is the first time." I said that it was my experience that children usually grieved for an absent parent, if not openly, then inside, as Billy seemed to be doing. I turned to Billy and said that I could tell that he missed his father. Mrs. Mosher said that Billy was only two-and-a-half years old when she and her husband separated. I said, "Then he is grieving for the father he wishes he knew."

I then told the boys that there was some adult business I wanted to discuss with Mr. Breslin and their mom. I showed them the way back to the waiting room and said we would meet together again in about thirty minutes.

When I returned, Mr. Breslin told me that the boys do not know it but that both boys were born before their mother got married. She said, "I married Jeff's father, not Billy's. The divorce decree states that no children were born to the marriage and that my husband denies paternity for both boys." I then said, "I guess I walked right into a family secret." Mrs. Mosher said the boys had witnessed her husband being brutal to her and she thought they remembered it. I said, "Even so, this does not stop children from hurting inside over an absent parent." Mr. Breslin wondered if the children shouldn't be told the truth. Mrs. Mosher expressed her wish that the boys not be harmed by having this information, that they not lose respect for her. I agreed, adding "This is a difficult

and delicate problem, but I am ready to help you with these decisions. Certainly the boys do not need to be told this week. It is
something you and I can explore together."

Mr. Breslin then said they really wanted help with the boys.
Last week, he and Mrs. Mosher went to the protective service
agency's psychologist right after they had an argument about jealousy. The psychologist had spent most of the time on the adults and
only talked to the children for fifteen minutes. Mr. Breslin said he
knew that he had a jealousy problem and that Marilyn had a lot of
need for male attention. He also said that he was an alcoholic who
had been sober for three years, and he had been "in treatment." He
then revealed that he was divorced and had two sons, each a year
older than Jeff and Billy, who lived in another state. I suggested
that we could work on both their own problems and the children's
problems. Mr. Breslin said that he would be okay, that what he
really wanted was help with the boys. I agreed that the boys would
be our focus. However, I also saw their concerns as a family problem and expected all of them to be involved. I explained that usually I interviewed all family members together, having found that
the most effective means for achieving rapid progress. At times, I
might also want to see family members individually.

Mr. Breslin expressed concern about the child protection
worker's use of the word "case" to describe them. He wanted to
know just what it meant that they were a "case." Did this mean he
was "labeled" as a child abuser in the computers and that this label
would follow him everywhere? I replied that my brief notes on the
referral from the child protection agency indicated that the abuse
was viewed as a one-time incident that was not likely to recur. However, if he did abuse a child again, the information might be re-
trievable. "Our counseling records are confidential," I said, adding,
"and the contents of our sessions are not going to be available in the
computers." The only exception would be if he were to again abuse
a child. Then I would have a legal responsibility to report it. I said,
"It is my impression that both of you are interested in getting help
for this family. How you got here is unfortunate. But I am hopeful
that we can resolve many of your concerns."

We discussed the time of future appointments. Because Mr.
Breslin's work schedule changes each week, the appointment times
would vary. I also told them that my vacation would begin in about
six weeks and suggested that we work hard on the family's problems
in the hope of making considerable progress before I left. At this
point, Mrs. Mosher explained that they too would be on vacation
for two weeks before I went.

I brought the boys back to the interview, telling them that I had been talking to their mom and Mr. Breslin about plans for our working together on family problems. I said, "I have learned from working with other families where there has been first a divorce and then new people becoming involved with the family, that there are many feelings about the divorce and then the new arrangements that need to be talked about. I think this is true of your family now. We will be working together for a few weeks now, and then again in the fall after school begins." I asked if they had any questions. I then confirmed our next appointment time and the interview ended.

A distinctive feature of this interview—one that on the face of it seems surprising—is the caseworker's deliberate avoidance of a discussion of the abusive treatment by Mr. Breslin that had precipitated the referral of the couple for counseling. Her decision to focus the interview on the children's behavior that had led Mr. Breslin to assault them physically is based on her primary goal in the interview: To engage the family members in a therapeutic counseling relationship. Achieving this goal would have been considerably more difficult if the worker had been accusatory or placed Mr. Breslin in the position of the "villain" responsible for the family's difficulties. Presumably, the circumstances surrounding the abuse had been thoroughly discussed during the protective worker's investigation. By "starting where the client is" and engaging these adults in an exploration of how they viewed their problem and how she may be helpful in its solution, the worker demonstrates that protective service and therapy are different processes. She establishes a therapeutic climate in which the clients can begin to work toward establishing more constructive family relationships.

The worker's choice of the children as the focus of attention in the very beginning of the interview serves to relieve the adults' unspoken apprehension about her anticipated criticism of them. Her sensitivity to the fears of all family members is also shown in her attempt to put them at ease by discussing what had been for them a happy event, the camping trip. She then directs the interview toward an examination of the boys' school adjustment and opens up the possibility that the adults do, indeed, need help in dealing with them.

Drawing on her professional experience and on her knowledge of children's emotional and developmental needs, the worker asks significant questions to direct the family toward the subject of family relationships. She explores, in particular, the boys' reaction to their own father and the fact that he is not living with them. The boys'

feelings about the absent father not only are emotionally of importance to the boys but also affect their relationship with Mr. Breslin.
By putting into words the inevitability of their grieving for their
father, the worker lets them know that she understands and empathizes with their unhappiness. She also "teaches" the adults that
the boys' missing their father is a normal and acceptable reaction,
and does not reflect unfavorably on either their mother or Mr.
Breslin.

Aware of Mrs. Mosher's discomfort when Mr. Breslin suggests
that there is something she should ask the worker, and correctly
assuming she is holding back because of the children's presence, the
worker, with a matter-of-fact, truthful explanation, takes them to
the reception room and assures them they will rejoin the adults.
When she learns the information the boys do not know, she acknowledges that her questions seemed to have precipitated dis-
closure of a "family secret" and gives the couple reassurance that
she will help them consider how best to tell the boys at some future
time.

It is noteworthy that Mr. Breslin, although identified as the
abuser of the boys, is the more active participant in the interview.
He demonstrates great interest in the children and seems to be trying to assume the role of father. The worker's response throughout
is one of accepting this couple and the children as a family unit,
which is the way in which they apparently view themselves. She
permits them to define the problems with which they need help and
assures them of her readiness to be helpful. At the same time she
refuses to be trapped into giving a facile or quick answer (as in their
request for advice about telling the boys the facts about their paternity) until she has established a firmer relationship with the family
members and knows them better.

This interview exemplifies the worker's ability to be sensitive to
the clients' feelings and at the same time to be firm in assuming
responsibility for helping the adults identify their need to work on
their problems. She sets the agenda, as it were, for the future counseling work to be done. In addition, she demonstrates her trustworthiness by being forthright about her responsibility to report Mr.
Breslin's abusive behavior should it be repeated. The extent to
which Mr. Breslin opens up in this interview, revealing a great deal
of important information about himself, combined with the readiness of the couple to accept further counseling attest to the worker's
achievement of her primary goal of engaging Mr. Breslin and Mrs.
Mosher in treatment of the family's problems.

15 "I would like Freddie to disappear— a terrible thing to say!"

Alleviating problems in a recently remarried family

The two interviews presented in this chapter are drawn from a family service agency's record of casework counseling with a husband and wife, married only two months, who were finding their relationship threatened and their home made chaotic during the weekly visits of the husband's son by his first marriage. This case illustrates skilled interviewing by an experienced caseworker in a type of family situation that is becoming increasingly common—the remarried family. In addition, the fact that this was so recent a marriage, the second for each partner, provided an opportunity for the caseworker to prevent the establishment or further aggravation of potentially destructive family relationships. This case was part of a research project that the agency was conducting on the remarried family as a distinct family system that appears to present family members with a specific set of relationship problems. The case demonstrates the need to integrate knowledge about this specific family situation with validated principles of casework interviewing.

The family included Fred Mansfield, thirty-two years of age, Sharon Mansfield, twenty-nine years of age, and Mrs. Mansfield's two sons, Skip, aged seven and one-half, and Chuck, aged six years. Freddie, five and one-half years old, lived with his mother, Mr. Mansfield's first wife. Mrs. Mansfield's first husband, the father of Skip and Chuck, maintained irregular and only brief contact with them. Although Mrs. Mansfield had said in her initial phone call to the agency that the problem was one of marital conflict, the first interview was held at her request with her alone.

Mrs. Mansfield explained that the reason for her request for an individual interview was to discuss her deep animosity toward her husband's son. Many of the marital problems she and her husband had revolved around this issue. Her husband felt that if she could get her feelings on this matter straightened out, there would be no other problems. Mrs. Mansfield thought that he was right. As Mrs. Mansfield made these remarks, she was troubled by shortness of breath and crying; she was unable to look directly at me and at times to continue with the conversation. I encouraged her to expand on her feelings. She described Freddie's behavior: He was destructive, unable to differentiate between what was his and what belonged to her children, did not obey her instructions, and was generally restless and impulsive. However, medical examination had ruled out hyperactivity. In contrast, her children were calm and fairly well ordered. They obeyed her and she felt in control of the situation when she was with them. Mrs. Mansfield hastened to clarify that her children were by no means perfect, but their misbehavior was normal and not wild as Freddie's was. She felt unable to reach Freddie and help him with his problems. I told her that this appeared to be a difficult situation. Mrs. Mansfield explained that she understood that there were many reasons for Freddie's difficult behavior, the most important of which was that he lived with his mother, who placed no limits on him.

I encouraged her to tell me more about the current living arrangement and visitation plan. Mrs. Mansfield explained that Freddie lived with his mother and visited in their home every weekend from Friday night to Sunday afternoon. In addition, his father saw him every Wednesday at his mother's home. Beyond this, he called Freddie on the telephone every night. Mrs. Mansfield went on to talk about the visitation arrangements her children have with their father and to contrast the difference in their experience with that of Freddie. She thought that another reason for her "animosity" toward Freddie was the feelings of jealousy she had because her children did not have an interested and involved father, and Freddie did. She described at some length the inconsistent pattern of visitation between her ex-husband and Skip and Chuck. Many Saturdays, they waited hours for him to show up and, when he did, he might spend only an hour or two with them. Although her children have accepted the undependability of their father, she knew that he had hurt them and she felt hurt for them. As she went on with this information, her irritation with her husband mounted and she expressed discomfort with his pattern of involvement with Freddie as "not right." With these feelings articulated, her agitation increased.

She said that if she did not work this problem out, so that she was not so irritated with her husband for his close relationship with Freddie, she feared that their marriage would not survive.

She changed the focus of the discussion to her deep feelings of self-doubt and the many mistakes she had made in her life, pre-dominantly in her first marriage. She was terrified that her present marriage also would fail. Her husband did not seem to understand her feelings or to support her in trying to work things out with Freddie. Yet, she said, her own self-doubts made her wonder if he was not right, even when her intuition told her that he was not. I said that she "had been through a great deal and it was understandable that she would feel these anxieties." Her capacity for introspection and her ability to look at her own role in the problem were clear, but I suggested that it was important to look at the whole picture and understand more fully what in the current scene she was react-ing to realistically. I said that these were things that we could work on together.

The worker's role up to this time is one of asking a few ques-tions to help Mrs. Mansfield expand on what is troubling her, to fill out the picture. The worker lets her know that she is sympathetic with her insecurities, particularly the remarriage, but begins to help her toward some consideration of contributing factors other than her animosity. The discussion that follows illustrates how appropri-ate validation can bring relief to clients and enable them to expand the focus of their discussion.

Mrs. Mansfield was very thoughtful for some time and then said that the thing that made her wonder the most about her behavior was that her husband was very patient with her children. He had "come on gradually" with her kids and really won them over. They felt very attached to him and he was "like another father to them." She added that he saw her as not trying so hard for his child. He also resented the fact that her children had a good mother and his child did not. I commented that earlier she had felt resentful be-cause Freddie got more from his relationship with his father than her children did from theirs; in a similar way it appeared that Mr. Mansfield felt that his son had less from his mother than her chil-dren do. Mrs. Mansfield agreed, but said that the problem was that she would like to be a better mother to Freddie, but it was very hard because of his bad behavior. When she was critical of Freddie's behavior, her husband put it in terms of "my children versus his child." She was afraid to make an honest observation because of this reaction. I asked a few questions to understand more about the discipline pattern in the home because it appeared to be a source of tension for Mr. and Mrs. Mansfield.

As the discussion continues, it becomes apparent that one of the key issues in the marital relationship is the matter of disciplining Freddie. The worker encourages Mrs. Mansfield to elaborate on this subject, because the issue of discipline, a here and now concern that is affecting the marital relationship, can also illuminate the dynamics of the parent-child and stepparent-child relationships.

Mrs. Mansfield revealed that her husband seemed unable to set any limits on Freddie and allowed him a free rein. She was the one who of necessity had to set limits. Then, when Freddie became angry about limits, his father came to his defense and found fault with her for administering the discipline. When these incidents happened repeatedly, she felt that things would never work out between her and her husband. "I would like Freddie to disappear, but that is not going to happen. It is a terrible thing to say."
I said that it was important to recognize her feelings and that together we could try to figure out ways to deal with them. I assured her that in this room, it was important for her to say what she felt. Mrs. Mansfield then added, "I have come to realize that Freddie will not disappear; it is not realistic. . . . He is not going to go away and I have to deal with my feelings." I recognized the mobilization of her energies in this direction and asked, "Where do we start?"

Mrs. Mansfield is direct about her frustration in dealing with her husband's son, the resultant dislike she experiences toward him because of this frustration, and her guilt about not being able to treat Freddie as her husband wants her to do. The worker sanctions the client's giving voice to her feelings, painful though it may be for her, and confirms the rightness of her facing the reality of her distressing emotions in the safe setting of the interview. Moreover, the worker explicitly states her willingness to help Mrs. Mansfield deal with those feelings, and, at the same time, permits her to choose which avenues she will explore.

Mrs. Mansfield repeated many of her frustrations with Freddie that she had talked of earlier in the interview. However, the inten-

sity of her feelings appeared to diminish and she commented that much of Freddie's behavior was normal for his age, if there was no consistent parent setting limits. She said that she resented her husband even more for not helping her with Freddie's discipline. She felt it unfair that she had total responsibility for his discipline. As we explored this subject, Mrs. Mansfield, with considerable understanding of her husband's dilemma, explained that this behavior was related to his guilt toward Freddie. I agreed with her observation. I said that there were many difficulties including finding ways to learn to live together, working out disciplining patterns for the child who visits, and dealing with feelings of guilt toward the child who does not live with you. I suggested that these were areas for further work. Mrs. Mansfield reported, however, that her husband did not think he needed help, that the problem was all hers. She, on the other hand, had had counseling and valued it. However, she acknowledged that he had said that he would be willing to participate in counseling if I thought it would be helpful.

In this segment the worker encourages full ventilation of feelings in order to relieve some of the internal pressure her client is under and increase her receptivity to her. Mrs. Mansfield was responsive to the worker's effort to shift the focus away from her absorption in her feelings of inadequacy and the marital conflict to a broader view of her situation as characteristic of many remarried families. Although not stating it in scientific terms, the worker introduced her to the idea of the remarried family as a specific kind of family system. It is also interesting to note that Mrs. Mansfield trusts the worker enough to reveal that her husband will come for counseling despite his earlier reported resistance.

The worker, in bringing the interview to a close, discusses the plans for involving the husband in the counseling process. Mrs. Mansfield's response indicates that the worker has succeeded in her goals of encouraging the expression of her painful feelings and deflecting her from self-blame to a more generalized view of her situation as characteristic of the remarried family system.

Throughout this interview, the worker combines appropriate confirmation of feelings with questions to reveal the nature and extent of the problem that brought the client to the agency. Moreover, the worker's security in directing the client's attention to the key issues to be dealt with is clearly seen. This "sureness of touch" comes from the worker's considerable knowledge of the remarried

family structure and its "built-in" stresses and her expertise in working with such families.

The second interview was a joint interview with Mr. and Mrs.
Mansfield. Mrs. Mansfield introduced her husband and said, "As
you can see, he decided to come with me." I expressed my pleasure
at seeing both of them and invited Mr. Mansfield to comment on his
feelings about coming. He said that he had discussed this rather
fully with his wife and knew that he could come in individually if he
wished. However, he thought it would be better to be seen together
rather than to "translate" for each other what was said. He really
did not know where to begin. I explained that there was no special
place to begin; it was important only to discuss what was important
to them.
Mr. Mansfield took the initiative and said that although he
knew that there were many things to discuss, he would like to start
with his wife's criticism of his relationship with Freddie. He pro-
ceeded to explain the reasons for this as Freddie's being the young-
est child in the house, Freddie's living with his mother, his limited
time with him, and his belief that the family should accommodate
Freddie's needs to a greater extent when he visited. He recognized
that Freddie was "a rambunctious little guy," and it was hard for
him to sit still. He speculated that when Chuck and Skip were Fred-
die's age, they were just as unmanageable, especially Skip. He was
discouraged because he and his wife had gone around and around
on this problem with no resolution.
I asked what he thought might be useful in dealing with the
situation. He said that he had discussed the situation with a doctor.
For a year or so after his divorce, he took Freddie with him wher-
ever he went and Freddie was very difficult to manage. He had been
assured by the physician that Freddie exhibited no abnormal be-
havior and ruled out the possibility of hyperactivity. He thought
that probably Sharon's children had also reacted to her divorce with
such behavior. He continued by describing his relationship with
Sharon's boys and said that he had no problems. However, initially
he had been nervous about how he would get along with them and
gradually established a positive relationship with them.
He recognized that his relationship with Freddie was different
from the one he has with Skip and Chuck. I asked how it was dif-
ferent. He said, "I baby him." He explained that he thought he
babied him because Freddie was younger than the other children in
the house and because his visitor status made him "low man on the

totem pole." He thought another part of the problem was that, by now, everyone was "nervous" when Freddie came to the house. He hoped that we could work on everyone not being so nervous around Freddie.

Mrs. Mansfield interjected, saying, "If Freddie behaved differently, no one would need to be nervous about his coming." She thought that this was the problem, and that her husband did not understand it. Instead, he blamed her because she reacted when Freddie "turned the house upside-down. Instead, you say it is my fault because I don't accept him." She did not expect Freddie to be an angel. She knew that all kids fight. The problem, as she saw it, was that she felt that Freddie should not be allowed to get away with as much as he did and her husband felt that he didn't get away with anything more than the other children. She argued that this simply was not true.

I reformulated the problem in terms of the different view on dealing with Freddie that each of them had as the major stumbling block in working things out, setting up tensions between husband and wife. Both agreed. I suggested that perhaps they could move away from a discussion of who was right and who was wrong and think together about what Freddie needed in order to be a calmer child. Inasmuch as there was no medical evidence to suggest a physical problem, it was important to recognize that Freddie's behavior was not only a problem for them as parents but could become a problem for him as he got older, if he did not get help with it now.

It is significant that both husband and wife have the same view of the source of the marital tension: conflict over how to discipline Freddie. The worker affirms the validity of their perception, and places it in the context of the need to consider what children need to grow and develop. The following discussion moves the interaction from one of a mutual blaming to a consideration of a parenting stance appropriate to the needs of all the children in the home.

Mr. Mansfield pursued the discussion of the deprivation he felt because Freddie did not live with him and his need "to make it up to him" when he did visit. I recognized his feeling and said that it was probably typical of many fathers in his situation. Mr. Mansfield acknowledged that the household was "a crazy scene" when Freddie came. The result was that he and Sharon had no energy for each other and instead argued about Freddie. He felt that their discussions went nowhere.

I agreed that it was a complex situation and suggested that our purpose would be to plan how to make things work better. And, with both of them together, we could begin this process. I suggested that our discussion would, of course, cover much of the material they had talked about with each other. I hoped, however, that I would be able to identify the roadblocks to resolution so that there would be a reduction of the tension that had brought them to the office. I went on to explain that there was work for each of them to do in resolving the problems about the discipline and integration of Freddie into their new family unit. I asked them to think together about what Freddie needed to grow up, rather than to blame Freddie or each other. The goal of this intervention was to move them away from the repetitiveness of blame and descriptive detail about Freddie's behavior to a consideration of the patterns that were going on in the household in relationship to Freddie. The greater gain for all family members would be a more harmonious household.

With this approach, Mr. Mansfield seemed to calm down and talked of how hard he had been trying, but he just had not known how to go about it. He felt that Freddie, at five, had so many disruptive things happen to him that he did not know how to handle telling him that his father had a new house and a new family. He knew that Freddie was jealous of his relationship with Skip and Chuck, especially when they called him Daddy. I agreed again that it was a difficult situation, hard on all family members, but I emphasized the positive aspects of a working family unit that served the needs of all. In a subdued way, Mr. Mansfield told of his efforts to make a go of his first marriage; he felt he had tried as much as he could. His sorrow was in leaving Freddie with his ex-wife, because he believed that she was not able to give him the training he needed. He felt unable to give Freddie enough on a visitation basis. He also felt that Freddie did not have a place in his new home.

Mrs. Mansfield assured her husband that Freddie did have a place in their home, if he were not so overindulged and if her husband could treat him as he did Skip and Chuck. She conveyed her understanding of the difficulty her husband was experiencing, but believed that his perception of the problem as her fault was simply not fair to her or to Freddie. She had shifted her focus from one of assumption of the total responsibility for the problems because of "animosity" to a perception of the problem in interactive terms between her husband, herself, and the children. She seemed less depressed and appeared to have more energy to engage in the problem-solving effort.

Mr. Mansfield admitted that he had often put his wife in the position of the "bad guy": He left the discipline to her so that he would not have to come down hard on Freddie when he was visiting. He felt overwhelmed because his decisions resulted in Freddie's not having a stable home. He said, "I wish I could make it different for him." I agreed with his wish and moved the focus to what would help Freddie the most. I acknowledged the past trauma of what had happened and the positive parenting efforts he had made. Mrs. Mansfield said that she knew that her husband wanted to be a good father and that she thought her animosity was really more anger at her husband because his problems, in working out his relationship with Freddie, were interfering with their marriage and chance of having a good family life.

The climate in the interview shifts from the repetitive reciprocal blaming pattern to a beginning awareness of the efforts of the other and the possibility of working out a mutual support system. Mr. Mansfield is able to acknowledge how well his wife sets flexible limits for her children and his wish that this could happen for Freddie. Mrs. Mansfield talks of her willingness and desire to do this for Freddie; however, she needs cooperation from her husband so that he is not angry with her. In addition, she needs her husband to set limits on Freddie rather than leave it all up to her. She praises her husband's role with her sons and asks that he relate in a similar way to Freddie. If that could happen, she feels she would not need to be the "bad" parent; nor would her husband come to Freddie's defense and reinforce her feelings that there is something wrong with her. The process of this discussion indicates that the different strands untangled in this interview are beginning to be rewoven in a coherent fashion. Thus, Mrs. Mansfield is able to articulate the basis for her so-called animosity in terms of patterns in the family system rather than internal pathology. With this relief to her self-concept, she is able to communicate to her husband her empathy for his plight and offers to function with him in a productive parenting relationship to facilitate Freddie's growth and enhance the total family unit. She volunteers the thought that, if Freddie is treated as Skip and Chuck are, it will give him a sense of greater belonging to this family unit so that he is not "low man on the totem pole."

Mr. Mansfield, on the other hand, while still protective of his involvement with Freddie and fearful that Freddie might lose out in this process, is beginning to recognize that the old patterns simply do not work and that new ones have to be developed. It is apparent that there are many issues that need to be dealt with in later interviews about his role with Freddie; however, the concept of an inter-active pattern has now been clarified and appears to be the one that has meaning to both partners.

The remainder of the interview was spent in expressions of mu-tual relief felt by each spouse because they had begun to really act on their problem rather than spin the repetitive themes of blame and self-defense. The worker affirmed their efforts to move in this direction and plans for other interviews were made.

Future work with this family will entail continued definitions of appropriate parenting roles and realistic expectations of each other in this area. The need for work with Mr. Mansfield in modifying his overclose relationship with his son has been clearly demonstrated in its detrimental effects on his son's development and in the forma-tion of the new family unit and marital tie. It appears that the work-ing through of this issue is crucial to the entire family unit. The worker has begun the process of loosening these restrictive parent-child bonds, harmful to both of them, and she appears to have achieved the dual goal of helping the husband move from projecting blame on his new wife and of engaging him in a consideration of the needs of his child and how best to nurture him. Also, Mrs. Man-sfield has made progress in shedding her burdens of guilt and self-blame.

These two interviews merit close study because they illustrate the interviewing skills developed by an experienced caseworker. For example, the worker is not trapped into taking sides in the argu-ment about disciplining Freddie, although there are points at which she might easily have been led to let these clients know which one was taking a sounder approach. She is able to be consistent in focus-ing not on the marital pair and their conflict but on the family as a whole and the remarried family in particular. And she shows self-confidence in being firm and forthright when these clients are strug-gling for a sense of direction. Finally, her exchange with these cli-ents is guided throughout by the very specific goals she wants to achieve with each of them.

Mr. and Mrs. Mansfield continued in weekly counseling ses-sions for four months. Mr. Mansfield made progress in lessening his overindulgence of Freddie, which was recognized as a reaction to his guilt about "deserting" him. Mrs. Mansfield became more hope-ful about the marriage and her initial depression was dispelled. Both Mr. and Mrs. Mansfield made progress toward stabilizing the mar-riage and Freddie became less impulse-ridden. The couple did not feel it was necessary for the worker to see the children—a point on which the worker concurred. These subsequent developments indicate that a destructive pattern of family relationships had indeed been broken and this remarried family had an improved chance of succeeding.

16 "There is always hope, you know"

Coping with a spouse's catastrophic illness

When catastrophic illness strikes a family, there is special need for a social worker's help to the patient and family members in coping with the initial shock and the continuing anxiety. Usually, additional stress is involved in planning for care after discharge from the hospital, especially if care away from home is indicated. Family members need information about and direction to resources in the community that can facilitate sound planning. In situations of terminal illness, the problems are exacerbated and family members' conflicting feelings can immobilize them, leading to the despair and depression illustrated in the following interview.

The family consisted of Saul Davidson, aged sixty-seven and retired, and his wife Lillian, aged fifty-seven. They had one son, married, who lived in the same city and maintained regular contact with his parents. Mrs. Davidson was gravely ill with cancer that had spread to other areas of her body. Several months previously, Mrs. Davidson had undergone surgery for breast cancer and had follow-up care in the chemotherapy clinic, where her condition was reported good. She resumed her active life socially and as a housewife. When, rather suddenly, her condition began to deteriorate rapidly, she had been readmitted to the hospital. The recommended plan following discharge was for full-time nursing care and Mr. Davidson was referred to the hospital's department of social services.

The social worker had had some brief interviews with Mrs. Davidson, who was disoriented a good deal of the time. At the time of this interview with her husband, she was completely incoherent.

126

Mr. Davidson, a short, heavy-set man, seemed overwhelmed by his wife's illness. He was friendly, but had had difficulty in expressing his feelings in the earlier interviews, which had consisted primarily of giving information about alternate plans of care. He avoided making specific plans but seemed inclined toward caring for his wife at home because that was her wish. However, he indicated in several comments that he was uncertain about such a plan.

Interview with Mr. Davidson—January 17

I interviewed Mr. Davidson today to find out what had taken place in his interview at The Cancer Foundation yesterday and to discuss discharge plans. Mr. Davidson came to see his wife as usual. He was sitting beside her bed, staring into his lap as I entered the room. His appearance was as usual: he was dressed neatly in a suit and tie.

As I came in, Mr. Davidson looked up and smiled. I asked him if we could go down to the solarium to talk and he agreed. As we were leaving, Mrs. Davidson mumbled something. We both paused as she continued, but her speech was unintelligible. Mr. Davidson seemed uncomfortable; he stood there in silence for a moment, fidgeting. I said sympathetically that I couldn't understand her. He smiled, shrugged, and said he couldn't either. We left the room together. Mr. Davidson smiles a lot when he is anxious, to cover his feelings or release them. He also seems a little shy and embarrassed when his feelings come out.

We sat next to each other in the solarium. I turned sideways to face him but our eye contact was infrequent. He glanced at me occasionally and looked down to his lap or out into the hall. I asked how his interview at The Cancer Foundation had gone. He said it went well; the people there were nice to him. But it did not seem they could do much for him. His wife needed a registered nurse twenty-four hours a day and he was told that they could not provide the nurses. They also told him that I would help him with that because he had to have a letter from the doctor. I explained that we did have to get a letter from the doctor for insurance purposes. If the need for a registered nurse was documented, his insurance would cover most of the cost and the foundation might be able to supplement the rest.

I said that I had spoken with Dr. Sachs about this problem and he was checking to see if he could justify a nurse around the clock. I asked Mr. Davidson if that was what he wanted. I explained what was involved procedurally with this alternative. I then asked him if this plan was still suitable to him because he had been uncertain. He

responded that he wanted whatever was best for his wife, and whatever Dr. Sachs thought would be best. After all, they were taking
good care of her here in the hospital. They had all the equipment
they needed here and taking care of her might be more difficult at
home. He just wanted what was best for his wife—that was the
important thing. I responded that I could see he wanted to do what
was best for his wife, but that it was also important to consider his
feelings. After all, he would be living there too if she came home
and needed twenty-four-hour help. He said, "That is true," but he
thought he would manage all right. They had a beautiful apartment,
with two bedrooms and a separate study near one of the bedrooms.
They had room for a nurse to move in and he wouldn't mind the
nurse's being there. He had been working on the study, cleaning it
up and moving things around in case his wife did come home. She
could stay in the study and the nurse could have the other bedroom.

He went on to say that if they told him Lillian was going to die
soon, he would go right ahead and bring her home. But the doctors
wouldn't give him a time limit and it might go on for months; that
really would be hard.

After a brief silence, he said that things had only gotten worse.
His wife had been doing so well until recently. She had been so
active—doing something all the time. Now she couldn't do anything. And she wasn't getting any better—only worse. Even with all
the medicine and everything they were doing for her, she was not
getting any better. She was suffering—he knew it. Mr. Davidson
became upset at this point and started to cry. He did not break
down completely, but his voice shook and there were many silences
when he had to stop talking to fight for control. He brought out his
handkerchief to wipe his eyes. His wife had always said that she
didn't want to be sick or ever be a burden to anyone—she wanted to
go fast when the time came. This is not how she had wanted things
to be. After another silence, he wiped his eyes, glanced at me and
smiled and said, "Now look at me, a grown man carrying on like
this. And you are just like a social worker, to sit there and just be
quiet, make me do all the talking till I put myself on the spot." I
asked if he felt on the spot when his feelings came out. He nodded
his head. I told him that I was quiet, not to make him talk or certainly not to make him feel on the spot, but to give him a chance to
talk about the things that were bothering him. He needed to let his
feelings out. What he was going through was hard, it was too much
to hold inside.

His comment was not hostile. He said it in a joking manner,
again trying to brush over his anxieties about having "let down" for

a few moments. I did not explore more into any underlying pattern of why he felt on the spot when his feelings came out. We were talking about his wife's death and I did not think it was appropriate. He had let down briefly, but his defenses had come back up and I respected his limits. I also feel that his comment was indirectly reaching out for feedback or some response from me.

Mr. Davidson said that his son had said that they really needed to sit down and talk about getting his wife home. But Lillian hadn't said anything about going home the last few days. He said we could wait and see what Dr. Sachs said about the letter, and as I had said before, he was the one that was going to be living there, he had to think about that, too. I agreed with him. I said that I would follow through with Dr. Sachs about the letter. Then I reminded him that we had talked about Mercy Hospital before as a back-up plan. In view of his wife's condition and the care she would need, I suggested that we should reconsider Mercy. Mr. Davidson said yes, but he just hated to think about Mercy. I asked why he hated to think about it. He said because it was the last stop. "The last stop?" I asked. Yes, he said, "When you go there that's it. When people go there they don't come out alive." I said, "And that's why you hate to think about Mercy, you fear that your wife won't come out alive?" He agreed, adding that he could not live without her and he became upset again. He had done everything for her. His job had been for her, all the money he ever made was for her. Everything was for her. There would be no reason for him to go on without her and he did not want to go on without her. He stopped talking and cried for a little while. His arm was resting on the armrest of his chair and I reached out and held his lower arm firmly for a few moments.

Mr. Davidson stopped crying and began talking about a new drug that was supposed to cure cancer that he heard about on the radio. He was going to talk to the doctor about it and tell him to give his wife some. "There is always hope, you know." He smiled and said that he could always hope for a miracle. I said that there was always hope but that his wife was very ill and had not been getting better; even though there might be hope, we had to deal with her condition as it was and make plans for her and for him. He said he knew that was true, he knew he had to make some realistic plans.

I told Mr. Davidson that I was going to speak with Dr. Sachs about the twenty-four-hour nurse and that I was also going to send in the Mercy Hospital application. He said okay, he would talk to Dr. Sachs as well. I said I would stop in to talk to him again soon. I

said that what he was going through must be so hard for him. I told
him to call me if there was anything I could do to help; I was always
available to talk to him.

The day following the above interview, Mrs. Davidson died.

The worker notes Mr. Davidson's upset and discomfort at his
wife's unintelligible speech. Although he smiles in greeting the
worker, it is apparent it is not easy for him to show his feelings or
articulate his pain. He seems to almost withdraw from contact. The
worker wisely begins with a question that relates to a practical matter—what he learned from an interview at an agency that might be a
resource in his planning. She keeps the focus on the need to plan
and tries to determine what he really wants to do. He continues to
emphasize that his wife's welfare is the important point. The worker
accepts this as what he wants and then points out the need to consider his feelings and the difficulties he might face in having his wife
at home. He tells her of his rearranging rooms in their apartment to
accommodate a live-in nurse. The worker's emphasis on considering
his needs also enables him to express how hard it would be if his
wife should require total care on a long-time basis.

Mr. Davidson is then able to express his concern for his wife
and his awareness that her condition is worsening. He cannot tolerate breaking down in the presence of the worker and tries to re-
cover by accusing her of remaining silent to put him "on the spot."
To Mr. Davidson, he has not demonstrated the proper behavior of
"a grown man." The worker does not interpret his remark as hostile, but as meant to be a joking comment. Whatever he meant, she
rightly asks if he feels "on the spot" when he expresses emotion.
Mr. Davidson nods agreement. The worker interprets his need, and
right, to express emotion in such a painful situation as his wife's
present illness. Sensitive to the reality that they are talking about his
wife's possible death, the worker does not pursue the topic of his
problem in expressing feelings.

When the worker suggests that they reconsider an alternative
plan previously discussed—placement in another hospital—he reveals his fear that going there means that his wife will die. After
telling of his devotion to his wife, and his not wanting to live without her, he cries. The worker expresses her sympathy silently.
When he recovers, he speaks of a new drug that he had heard of
and his plan to ask the doctor to give it to his wife. His need to
retreat from the thought of his wife's death is further shown in his
expression of "hope for a miracle." The worker's supportive response accepts his need to hope while at the same time she helps

him stay with the reality of the situation and he responds with agreement. The worker, in ending the interview, reviews what she will do and assures him of her availability, recognizing the pain he is feeling.

The worker's concern about Mr. Davidson's depression naturally increased when she learned of his wife's death. She noted in the record her plan to contact him, although she was not sure he would be receptive to further contact with her. She telephoned Mr. Davidson, who refused an interview, stating he could not return to the hospital. The worker telephoned him a few more times. A month later, he came to see her after she had explained that her office was in an annex, not in the hospital building. It was a most painful interview for both of them. Mr. Davidson's expression of his extreme grief and his continuous talk of suicide were overwhelming to the young worker. Despite her own pain, she handled the interview well and helped Mr. Davidson agree to an appointment in the hospital's psychiatric service. He saw the psychiatrist, who confirmed his severe depression. Mr. Davidson refused further treatment, but later agreed to having two telephone contacts a week with the worker. When he learned months later that she would be leaving the hospital for another position, he withdrew from telephone contacts. Weeks later, however, he initiated and maintained weekly telephone calls with the worker's supervisor, whose name he had been given. Frequently, he referred to "still missing" the worker.

The follow-up report is, in this instance, truly poignant, illustrating the value of a relationship with an understanding person during a time of great crisis. A man who tended to be inarticulate, and, under extreme stress, become depressed, was able to accept a limited contact with persons whom he knew cared about him and wanted to be helpful. The hospital, a symbol of the loss of his wife, also came to represent a place where he could, again to a limited extent, maintain a contact that offered him some comfort and support in his bereavement.

17 "I don't have an anger problem. My wife runs around"

Beginning treatment of abusive behavior

The three interviews recorded in this chapter and in chapters 18 and 19 concern instances of domestic violence. The source of this material is a family service agency that had a special arrangement with a domestic relations court whereby the agency accepted as clients those abusing spouses who had been ordered by the court to seek counseling help.

The interview below is the first, or intake, interview with a thirty-four-year old man ordered by the court to see a family service agency worker as an alternative to a jail sentence for violent behavior toward his wife. He is living with his second wife, the mother of their two children. The court indicated that his abusive behavior, which has erupted about five times in the past few years, was only moderately severe.

WORKER: *I'm glad you found the office without much of a problem. As I recall from our phone conversation last week, you are under obligation to the court to come here.* (Worker directly acknowledges the nonvoluntary, forced nature of Joe's application. Joe needs to know that the worker recognizes he is here under duress and will permit him to express the resentment he feels.)

JOE: *The court ordered me here, and I'm not too damn happy about it.*

WORKER: *Beats jail, but just barely?*

JOE: *You said it!*

WORKER: *What does the court require? Letters or reports or what?*

JOE: *It's a six-month, informal pretrial probation-type deal. They need regular reports.*

WORKER: *Well, that's pretty much the standard deal. I'll start sending reports as of today. I don't think that'll be a problem. Do you see any problems with our meeting weekly and sending the reports?* (Worker invites Joe to participate in the planning—one technique for laying the foundation for a working relationship. Moreover, the worker knows that Joe will be worried about the contents of the report, because they will influence the judge's decisions.)

JOE: *I don't know about this time of day. My job is new and I get all the worst hours—call ins—all the junk.*

WORKER: *We can pick a time and change as we go along if there are unexpected problems.* (Worker makes it clear that he is flexible and will try to accommodate Joe, to make it possible for him to meet the court's requirements.)

JOE: *You do this a lot?* (Client does a little testing to discern whether the worker is competent and therefore potentially helpful.)

WORKER: *I've worked with anger in marriages a lot.* (Worker uses a direct approach and identifies the client's central problem, based on his professional knowledge of the key issues in violent behavior.)

JOE: *I don't have an anger problem. My wife runs around.*

WORKER: *What do you do about that?* (Worker explores the client's situation as he sees it, fact-gathering as a basis for understanding the client's unique circumstances and his reactions. He permits the client to deny that anger is a problem for him. To get into an argument with a client so early in the contact would retard the establishment of a therapeutic relationship.)

JOE: *I keep a record.*

WORKER: *That's got to be rough, Joe.* (Worker conveys to the client his appreciation of the client's probable feeling, thus strengthening the beginning working relationship.)

JOE: *Fifty times, she's stayed out all night.*

WORKER: *That's rough, all right. What do you do about it?*

JOE: *I've tried everything. I can't please her. What's the matter with her, anyway?*

WORKER: *Sounds frustrating for you.*

JOE: *Makes me mad as hell sometimes.*

WORKER: *Is that how you got to court?* (Worker turns the client's attention back to the reality of the court referral, which is the framework within which both client and worker must operate.)

JOE: *Driving along in the car, I'm talking about us, she gets sore and grabs the wheel.*

WORKER: *While you're on the freeway?*

JOE: *Right! I slapped her. Man, she could have killed us both!*

WORKER: *That sounds like a pretty big fight. Do you two fight like that often?* (The worker does more fact-gathering to build a realistic picture of the probable nature and extent of the abuse. He encourages Joe to think about the circumstances that seem to precipitate his violent reactions.)

JOE: *Four, five times in the last few years.*

WORKER: *That kind of fight must be hard on both of you.*

JOE: *I hate them!*

WORKER: *Are they always about her running around?*

JOE: *No. Money sometimes.*

WORKER: *Anything similar about the fights?*

JOE: *They're always bad.*

WORKER: *Always physical?*

JOE: *No, words mostly.*

WORKER: *Words can be very painful.*

JOE: *We're both mean when we drink.*

WORKER: *Like two different people?*

JOE: *Right! We're good when we're not tanked up. . . . Listen, what kind of reports do you have to send?* (Excessive drinking is probably a central factor in Joe's behavior and his wife's, too. His sudden shift to a different subject is a clue that a particularly sensitive area has been touched. Or it may indicate that the worker has failed to discuss sufficiently the content of the reports and Joe's reaction to them.)

WORKER: *When you come, how regularly, and how well you're doing handling your anger.* (Worker gives a direct, nonevasive answer, again putting his finger on the core issue of anger. Joe's response this time shows less resistance to the worker's interpretation and less need to deny his hostility.)

JOE: *Oh. She's damn mean too!*

WORKER: *When you both drink it's World War III.*

JOE: *Right! That's when she takes off, too.*

WORKER: *Maybe both of you could learn how to handle fights and anger better?* (Worker verbalizes that this is a mutual problem of husband and wife, not Joe's alone.)

JOE: *Maybe. I think she'll come here, too.*

WORKER: *That will really help. It sounds like both of you would like to have a more peaceful marriage.*

JOE: *We get along good most of the time.*

WORKER: *That's a good foundation for us to build on.*

JOE: *Okay. I've got to come anyway.*

WORKER: *Yes, and if things get better you win both ways.*

(Worker tacitly accepts Joe's continued resistance but does not permit him to escape from the reality of having to continue counseling both to avoid going to jail and potentially to improve the marital relationship.) *Maybe now is a good time to get some general background stuff from you—date of birth, job, kids, and so forth.*

JOE: *Okay, but what's it for?*

WORKER: *Mostly for our records but also it helps me in my work to know some general background material.* (The worker's honesty and nonevasion in answering Joe's suspiciousness should reassure him that the worker is trustworthy. A fifteen-minute period of history-taking followed.)

WORKER: *You left home when you were sixteen years old. That's really quite a big move for a teenager.* (Worker shows appreciation of Joe's early unhappiness and his strength in taking action to improve his life.)

JOE: *It was, but a lot better than home.*

WORKER: *That's a rough decision for a teenager to have to make.*

JOE: *Like I said, anything was better.*

WORKER: *Lots of fights?*

JOE: *The two of them fought all the time.*

WORKER: *Physical fights?*

JOE: *He drank, he yelled, he hit.*

WORKER: *So he beat up on everybody when he drank.*

JOE: *He and Mom fought and drank every week.*

WORKER: *I guess I can see why you left.* (Worker undoubtedly sees the similarity between the parental behavior Joe reported and his current behavior, but he does not feel it would be useful so early in the contact to call this similarity to Joe's attention. Probably this will be dealt with at a later time.)

JOE: *I did all right. I got two skilled trades and even finished high school in the army.*

WORKER: *You have a right to feel good about all that. You really did it all by yourself.* (Reality-based ego support is strengthening.)

JOE: *I can do most things I really try to. I'm a loner and I've learned to do it myself. Don't take anything, from anybody!*

WORKER: *Independence is a good thing these days. It's good to be able to stand up for yourself and to have some close people to share with.*

JOE: *Yeah. I think that's right too. Sometimes you have to be hard.* (Joe "hears" the part about independence but not about sharing and closeness.)

WORKER: *Sure. Anger management is like using a flashlight rather than a floodlight. Learning some safe ways to show anger at home, for example.*

JOE: *So what time next week?*

WORKER: *Same time. Let's have your wife in, too. We can start working on those things that keep you two apart.* (Worker sets the pattern for future contacts and makes clear to Joe that the problem is shared by his wife, without directly saying so.)

JOE: *Okay—that sounds okay.*

18 "He always does that to me, traps me"

Treating marital conflict

The interview in this chapter is the fifth held with a couple in their mid-thirties who have been married for fifteen years. Max, age thirty-seven, has a master's degree in business administration and is employed in a well-paying management position. Jan, age thirty-four, is also a college graduate. They have three children, two sons, five and ten years, and a daughter, seven years. Max's abuse of Jan had occurred five times in the past year and was considered moderately severe.

The previous interview had dealt with the couple's level of stress and their coping capacities. Also dealt with was Max's tendency to make unrealistic demands on his family. In this case, the worker used as tools in his work with the couple the "SUDs scale," drawn from assertion training. ("SUDs" stands for subjective units of distress and is measured subjectively by the client on a scale of 10 to 100. Each increment represents the heightening of anxiety and tension.) The worker's aim was to promote the clients' awareness of the stress they experience and to teach them specific techniques—such as exercise, diet, relaxation, scheduling, and taking time out—for lowering the stress level and managing stress more effectively. His method is educational and, therefore, his interviewing technique is highly active and directive.

WORKER: *How were your stress levels this week? Did either of you have problems rating your SUDs levels?* (Worker takes the initiative in setting the agenda for this session, which is to be further work on stress and how to manage it.)

MAX: *Basically, a good week. I have found the daily exercise a bit frustrating, a bit hard physically as well, but I think it may be beneficial.*

WORKER: *Jan, you look upset. How was the week for you?* (Worker acknowledges Jan's nonverbal communication of dissatisfaction and pushes her to talk about it.)

JAN: *It was fair. Max has been better—we have made time to talk and even engineered a night out.*

WORKER: *But?*

JAN: *He got upset about the kids early in the week.*

WORKER: *How upset were you, Max?*

MAX: *Children need to learn responsibility. I believe responsible parenting requires consistent, determined action. Respect, proper behavior, and good manners are basic requirements. Any good mother should want these things. Jan is a good mother, perhaps lax.* (Max evades a direct answer to the worker's query about his feeling of stress, the intended focus of the interview. Instead, he talks about the precipitating episode, the conflict over the children.)

WORKER: *How much stress? How upset were you, Max?*

JAN: *He yelled for two days—Hitler personified.*

MAX: *If you had done what I asked, this would not have happened.*

WORKER: *Time out. Let's take five minutes to breathe deeply and relax.* (Worker takes charge and models the stress management techniques he has been teaching them to use in conflict over the children.)

WORKER: *Now, you both were about to begin a fight about the fight—that's a "no-win" fight and a very high cost use of anger. This seems like a long-term fight—a fight that creates a great deal of stress and upset. How upset were you, Max?* (This is the third time the worker has tried to bring the interview focus back to Max's upset.)

MAX: *The whole thing makes me mad as hell. She . . .*

WORKER: *Just mad?*

MAX: *Frustrated—frustrated and angry.*

WORKER: *Frustration and anger are a volatile combination. I can see why you were so upset. As a businessman, Max, and an administrator, you're used to pragmatic thinking: results are the key to success.* (Worker refers to Max's area of expertise to further his engagement in an analysis and clarification of his reactions.)

MAX: *Of course; how does this apply?*

WORKER: *Long-term problems are often the result of a lack of creative solution application. The problem remains because couples try to use the same ineffectual solution.*

MAX: *There is a right way and a wrong way . . .*

JAN: *And yours is always the right way!*

WORKER: *Time out! Aren't we mistaking methods and goals? Responsibility, for example, is an almost universal goal of parenting, but the timetable and the method can be flexible. Jan, Max, what is important, the end result or the process, the method?*

JAN: *The result.*

MAX: *The success, depending upon its cost.*

WORKER: *Yes, cost. The current solution doesn't give a positive result and its cost is high. The cost is emotional, you both feel upset about this issue and even grow apart, frustrated, resentful.*

MAX: *Okay, that's valid.*

JAN: *It depends on how it's done, Max. You . . .*

WORKER: *Wait, Jan, we have agreement about flexibility, that's important, and we can only deal effectively with one issue at a time. Max, let's go back to your phrasing, to your tone in describing the problem. (Worker paraphrases Max's statements and Max agrees to the accuracy.) How did Max's statements make you feel, Jan?*

JAN: *Mad.*

WORKER: *Not compliant, not concerned, not receptive?*

JAN: *Mad, disgusted, rebellious. He always does that to me, traps me.*

MAX: *Wait, wait! This is not fair, not accurate. I stated the problem simply. I don't see any trap there. The solution is simple, simplistic!*

WORKER: *Max, your goals are good. Something doesn't work out, however. The method isn't effective. Jan felt trapped and therefore rebellious—perhaps the rhetorical question you asked is the weak link? (Worker validates Max's goals but points out the ineffectiveness of his method.)*

MAX: *I don't follow this.*

WORKER: *Rhetorical questions don't invite discussion. Good parents want their children to be responsible, clean, well-behaved, and so on, but not everyone agrees about how and when this can be accomplished. If Jan were to disagree with you, she would set herself up as a bad parent. If she agrees with your goals—well, then, she feels compelled, trapped, into agreeing with your method.*

MAX: *Just good debate.*

WORKER: *Unquestionably, Max. Effectual problem solving isn't always the same as good debate, however.*

JAN: *I do feel trapped and like I'm in a debate, Max. I've never disagreed about the goals, just the means to the end.*

WORKER: *Positive results, solutions, teamwork.*

MAX: *This can't be solved overnight. I think there is something here. The technique, my method may not be. . . .*

WORKER: *Effective.*

MAX: *Effective. Yes. Solutions are more important.*

WORKER: *Great. Now, let's put the kids on the shelf for three weeks while we deal with problem-solving techniques. It's probably not realistic to try to solve this type of problem without more time and perspective. Let's go back to stress and anger. The higher a person's stress level, the higher the possibility for anger outburst.* (Worker feels that the argument about childrearing cannot be solved in this interview and that it is more important to concentrate on the key issues of stress and anger. Therefore, he takes the lead in redirecting the discussion.)

JAN: *Yes, I see that. When I'm anxious, under stress, I can get angry with the kids or Max or whoever, almost spontaneously.*

MAX: *I suppose that's true of everyone.*

WORKER: *Yes, I agree, Max. Stress is an anger activator for us all. Sometimes the very things that anger us are stressful, stressors. So stress can cause us to be angry and can cause us to be more angry or less effectively angry.*

MAX: *So the kids are a source of stress, stressors. Yes, they also make me more angry, upset, even if they aren't the direct cause.*

WORKER: *Okay, that's good awareness. Awareness of stress and stressors is a first, the first step to power and control. So first we avoid the stress if possible—in this case, avoid the kid issues, not to escape, but to gain knowledge and perspective.*

MAX: *This won't go away by avoiding it.*

JAN: *He's not saying avoid, he's saying. . . .*

WORKER: *Time out! A three-week time out from the parenting* problems—definitely not a permanent dropping of the issue. Both of you have valid points. We won't avoid these issues, just gain some technical knowledge. I'm sure the problems will still be there.

JAN: They will be there, and yes, I think Max is right. I mean, there are problems.

MAX: Well, yes. I think we agree. Okay, three weeks is good.

WORKER: So stress management—exercise, diet, relaxation, scheduling time out. . . .

MAX: Do you have this written out?

WORKER: You are a mind reader, Max. Lists, how to's, you'll have a bookful soon. Here's the first installment.

JAN: I think I've read some of this recently.

WORKER: Stress management has been getting a lot of attention lately. You probably have seen most of this before.

WORKER: Let's think about expectations in this context. Very high expectations can create a lot of stress. Sometimes, people's expectations shift and change, creating even more stress. Sometimes, people don't clearly state their expectations. (Worker pursues the educational approach he finds most helpful in this type of problem.)

MAX: I think I am sometimes less clear than I perhaps should be.

WORKER: How about you, Jan? Are you clear? Have you noticed Max sometimes not being clear?

JAN: I think I am pretty clear. I think I feel uncertain a lot about what Max wants.

MAX: Okay, I buy that. I think you are clear when you finally say things. But I don't think you always say what you think, or tell me what you want.

JAN: I guess I'm so worried about being a nag that I don't say enough.

WORKER: It seems that you both have learned about some things that each of you could work on that would improve communication and reduce some stress and maybe anger in your marriage. Do either of you ever feel frustrated when your expectations are not met—angry and frustrated because he or she does not do it properly?

MAX: Well, yes. Naturally, anyone would feel frustrated and angry in that kind of situation. I think I feel that way because it's a perpetual occurrence.

JAN: You demand too much, the children are too young to do some of the things you ask, and you allow no margin for error.

MAX: *I only ask what I think, and believe, to be proper—what was expected of me.*

WORKER: *Perhaps too much, too soon, was asked of you, Max. As we said earlier, the goals sound realistic but the methods don't seem to work. This is sort of a human engineering problem; we need to lower the cost and raise production. Let's pick this up next week. Let's take time out now, relax and think of a positive experience the two of you had together recently. . . . Now that you both have an experience in mind, I'd like you, Max, to begin by telling Jan how good you feel about this experience and how good you feel toward Jan.* (Worker shifts the discussion away from problem solving to a review of a positive experience. When an interview can end on a warm note, there is more likelihood of positive carryover to the couple's relationship between interviews.)

MAX: *Jan, you made me feel very good when I think about our evening together.*

WORKER: *Max, I think you're making a very good effort. I know this is hard and rather strange for most people at first. Max, try starting with an "I" statement about how you felt.*

MAX: *I feel, felt very happy Thursday night. I liked the attention and the affection you gave me.*

WORKER: *That is perfect. You're really getting all of this very quickly, Max. Jan, how do you feel about what Max just said?*

JAN: *I feel very warm, very good. Thank you, Max.*

WORKER: *That was a very positive, warm response and a very good response, clean, to Max's compliment. Now, Jan, tell Max how you felt about your remembered experience.*

JAN: *I felt very loved, very desired by you Thursday night. I just. . . .*

WORKER: *Stop, Jan. Don't qualify or limit your statement. Positives are more effective in reinforcing behavior than negatives.*

MAX: *Thank you, let's do it again.*

It is interesting to note that Max's violent behavior is never mentioned, though it is the overt reason for the couple's contact with the counseling agency. An obvious characteristic of this interview is the active role taken by the interviewer. Undoubtedly, this activity was made possible by the fact that a working relationship had already been established. By the fifth interview, the worker had a great deal of information about the couple and could be sure of the direction in which it would be helpful for them to move. Contrast the worker's activity here with that of the previous interview, which was the first interview with the client.

19 "I feel more relaxed about being a man"

Learning to control anger

The following interview took place near the end of a four-month counseling contact with a twenty-eight-year-old man who had been involved only in individual, twice-a-week counseling interviews. Brad is a college graduate, a businessman who is separated from his wife pending a divorce. His abusive behavior had occurred only twice and had been labeled mild by the court.

WORKER: *How was the week?*

BRAD: *Fair. No anger problems. Mild stress. Two dates, and no problems sleeping.*

WORKER: *So what made it just fair?*

BRAD: *That's the good part. The bad part was a dent in the car, and a bad phone call from my wife.*

WORKER: *Some bad, but mostly good, Brad.*

BRAD: *Yes, you're right. Focus on the positives and don't dwell on the downers. At least I'm learning—I didn't say it was a bad week!* (Client is proud of the progress he has made and wants the worker to acknowledge that he is doing well.)

WORKER: *Top of the class. I don't blame you for being down about the car and the call. How did you handle them? What were your feelings?* (Worker gives positive reinforcement to client's statements.)

BRAD: *It's funny, I didn't get angry about the car. It was an "act of God" problem and therefore out of my control. So, instead of yelling and kicking the car, I called the insurance man, got two estimates, and played three games of racketball with Dave.*

WORKER: *You are fantastic. That was using anger positively and*

144

constructively. Dave—is he the guy you met playing softball? (Further approval based on Brad's genuine improvement in handling his anger.)

BRAD: *Yes. Socialize and exercise. I can't believe it. I like it, I like me.*

WORKER: *It sounds like a lot of people agree about that from what you've said this last couple of months.*

BRAD: *I'm getting there and, well, I like it. I feel more accepted, acceptable.*

WORKER: *You're more positive, more controlled, more discriminating with your behavior.* (As counseling draws to a close, the worker verbalizes the client's gains, which have been substantial enough so that Brad is deemed ready to stand on his own feet.)

BRAD: *No more "stress man."*

WORKER: *So what about the phone call?*

BRAD: *Definitely a 70 on the stress scale.*

WORKER: *How angry were you?*

BRAD: *Heated up, but I used lots of positive self-talk. Tried to focus issues, the whole anger management routine.*

WORKER: *And?*

BRAD: *The lady doesn't always fight fair.*

WORKER: *What did you do?*

BRAD: *Took a time out. "Call you later, this is not a good time to talk, I'm uptight." This is still very hard to do, I still think in win/lose terms with her.* (Client affirms his behavioral gains but also acknowledges that he has further progress to make.)

WORKER: *It's hard, but you're doing well. You could have fallen into a real fight. Maintaining control is always the effective, powerful thing.* (Worker accepts the client's statement, which is more supportive than if he had given false assurance that Brad had completely conquered his anger.)

BRAD: *It's a lot easier with other people.*

WORKER: *Very true. Of course if you can do it with her. . . .*

BRAD: *I can do it, period.*

WORKER: *I think you're beginning to read my mind.*

BRAD: *It's one-track!*

WORKER: *Think so? How were the dates?* (Worker rounds out the termination by inquiring about the client's man-woman relationships—an important area for a person who is separated and awaiting divorce.)

BRAD: *Good. Women today are different.*

WORKER: *How are they different?*

BRAD: *More aggressive sexually, more assertive, maybe more ac-*
   cepting, too.
WORKER: *A lot depends on the man. You're different now.*
BRAD: *Yes, and that's true. I wouldn't—didn't believe I could*
   handle being single—losing her. Dating really isn't so bad;
   women want different things than I thought. I feel pretty secure
   now—I mean I feel more relaxed about being a man.
WORKER: *The "iceman" thaws! You are really aware, really in*
   control but open.
BRAD: *I feel good about it. I think I know who I want to be.*

One is impressed with the "lightness of tone" of both client and worker throughout this interview, which testifies to the success of the counseling experience and the use the client has made of the counselor's help.

20 "She makes me feel so guilty"

Achieving emotional emancipation in adolescence

The three interviews in this chapter illustrate the interviewing process over a fifteen-month period with an unhappy adolescent girl who is struggling to move from her childhood dependencies to independent adulthood. Presented here are the first interview, the twenty-third, which was a joint interview with the mother and daughter midway through the counseling, and the forty-ninth interview, which was the final interview with the girl.

The first contact with Sue Allen was arranged through the public high school social worker. A seventeen-year-old junior, Sue had voiced concern about her mother's chronic illnesses and her own difficult home life. Feeling that Sue was probably a good candidate for sustained counseling, the school social worker referred her to the family agency which offered an "outreach to teens" self-referral counseling service.

An attractive girl with a slim figure and short, wavy hair, Sue arrived promptly for her first interview. She was smiling brightly, but almost immediately I sensed a feeling of anxious despair underneath the cheerful and lively facade. When I mentioned that the school social worker had told me of her mother's chronic illnesses, her cheerfulness all but disappeared and sadness emerged.

SUE   *(speaking in a high, anxious tone): I just don't understand it. I never have. It seems she's been sick in bed with all sorts of things all my life. I don't know what's wrong with her. (In an angry, almost desperate tone) She has never told me what her real trouble is. I just know, whatever it is, it has incapacitated* her. It's gone on since I was six years old—that's when my father died of cancer. But it seems as if it has gotten worse since I was about twelve—that's five years now.

WORKER: *It must seem almost unbelievable to you.* (Worker responds to Sue's desperation, not to the reality of the situation she is describing.)

SUE: *Yes! If she was really sick, wouldn't she tell me what is wrong? She's always complaining but she doesn't take care of herself the way she should if she's really sick!*

WORKER: *What do you mean by that, Sue?* (Worker conveys to Sue her interest in truly understanding the problem by asking her for more details.)

SUE: *Well, for instance, she'll fix herself a meal and then complain that she didn't feel well enough to do it—lots of things like that.*

WORKER: *And how does that make you feel?*

SUE: *It makes me so frustrated. And I feel guilty, too, as if I never can do enough for her.*

Sue then talked about things being worse in the past few years because her sister had married and left home, and she and her mother had moved into the maternal grandmother's home to save money.

SUE: *At first I thought it would be great because I thought my grandmother could be my mother now, and take care of me, and make meals for me and go to things with me as I had wanted my mother to do. But all that happened was that my grandmother slowly got sick of my mother's always being in bed and just began to complain to me about her not doing any work!*

WORKER: *Sounds like you've been carrying an awfully big burden. It must feel pretty overwhelming at times.* (Worker continues to let Sue know she empathizes with her feeling of despair and frustration.)

SUE *(sadly and looking close to tears):* It sure does.

WORKER: *Well, maybe that's where I can help. Sometimes things don't feel so overwhelming if you talk about them with someone outside the situation.* (Worker begins to define the nature of counseling help.)

SUE *(with a look of skepticism):* I don't see how talking about it will help. The whole thing has been going on for years and it's all on me and I don't think it's going to change.

WORKER: You are right that it's been going on for a long time, but that doesn't mean that things may not change. (Worker recognizes Sue's resistance.) Maybe if we work together we can see if some of your problems can be resolved.

SUE: Well, maybe. I guess it wouldn't hurt to try.

There followed a long pause in the conversation which the worker did not interrupt, permitting Sue to contemplate her thoughts. Suddenly, Sue spoke up in a newly angry tone.

SUE: I tried so hard to find out what was the matter with my mother. I told her I had to know. She was her usual vague self. So then I asked her if I could call her doctor, and she finally said yes. I called him, and guess what he said! He said he couldn't give me any information—I would have to ask my mother!

WORKER: That's understandable, Sue. A doctor has to respect the confidential nature of information about a patient. Just as I would never give information about you to anyone unless you gave your consent. Maybe you could ask your mother if you can accompany her to a doctor's appointment and let the doctor explain her illness to you in her presence. Finding out about your mother's illness seems to be very important to you. (The worker accomplishes two things. She reinforces the sense of her own trustworthiness in respect to not giving others information about Sue. She also responds to the urgency of Sue's expressed need by suggesting a way it can be met.)

SUE: Yes, because of my father. Nobody ever told me that my father was sick. Then, all of a sudden, he died and I wasn't ready for it. Maybe that will happen to my mother, too. But I have to be ready for it.

After this expression of what was a most terrifying idea, Sue immediately changed the subject and began to talk about her sister's having moved out of the home, although she still lives in the area. Recognizing the pain she was experiencing, I allowed her to talk without interruption. The sisters still have a close relationship and Sue goes to visit her sister when she feels blue.

WORKER: It's important to have someone who will listen, isn't it?

SUE: It always makes me feel better.

WORKER: It sounds to me as if you have a lot to handle and I'd like to help you handle some of it. How about our meeting *once a week to talk about these problems and see if we can't resolve some of them?* (The worker suggests a plan for continued counseling but permits Sue to express her reaction.)

SUE: *I guess that's okay. My mother already knows I planned to talk with a social worker and she thinks it's all right.*

WORKER: *Right now, we can plan weekly appointments. But something we might think about for the future is also having your mother and grandmother come in to discuss some of these problems. (Sue frowned.) You look as if you are uncertain this is a good idea, Sue, but it is all really too much for you to handle alone. They need to share the problem so they can be part of the solution.* (Clearly, the worker sees this as a parent-child relationship problem for which both the mother and the daughter need to be involved if there is to be improvement. She lets Sue know her ideas about this but does not insist on immediate action.)

Assessing the significance of this initial interview, the worker notes from the outset that one of her crucial functions is to *listen.* Sue has felt unheard for years. Potentially, at least, the worker will be someone who will be there only for Sue. Her frustration, anger, and desperation were natural responses to her feeling of being neglected. To the worker, they represented a cry for help. The resistance Sue shows so clearly is her way of testing the worker to be sure she is really "with" Sue. To make appropriate responses, the worker has to be aware not only of Sue's words but also of her tone of voice and her nonverbal gestures. It also means giving verbal support to Sue as she begins to expose negative feelings she has long suppressed, as well as gently asking questions that will help to clarify the issues Sue needs to face.

Two issues, dependence and guilt, are central ones for Sue. And it is these issues that formed the core of Sue's problem in her relationship with her mother. In subsequent interviews the worker's aim will be to help Sue develop a sense of control over her own decision making through experiencing the worker's sustained support.

Between the initial interview and the twenty-third, a portion of which is reproduced below, Sue made progress in being able to express the anger, frustration, and disappointment in her mother that she had repressed since childhood. Her growing ability to acknowledge these feelings increased her determination to confront her mother. Several family interviews in which Mrs. Allen and her mother, Mrs. Haines, were included, served as a testing ground for

Sue where she was able slowly and cautiously to expose her feelings. The twenty-third interview included Sue, Mrs. Allen, and the worker. The previous interview had also included Mrs. Haines.

MRS. ALLEN *(the first to speak): I think it's better not to have my mother here.*

WORKER: *Why is that?*

MRS. ALLEN: *Because she just causes more trouble than she's worth and is so bitchy.*

WORKER: *It seems to me that she acts bitchy because she is disappointed.* (Worker acknowledges client's description but puts it in a different perspective.)

SUE: *In me?*

WORKER *(addressing both Sue and Mrs. Allen): What do you think?*

MRS. ALLEN *(in a condescending tone): Well, I know she is.*

WORKER: *What about?*

MRS. ALLEN: *I know exactly what she's disappointed about. She's disappointed in the fact that Sue is a very bright child but doesn't use her capabilities. She's also disappointed that Sue doesn't know when to bite her tongue.*

WORKER *(sensing Mrs. Allen's denial of her mother's disappointment in her): Do you think she's only disappointed in Sue?*

MRS. ALLEN: *No, she's disappointed in me, too.*

WORKER: *How do you think she's disappointed in you?* (Worker encourages this revelation because she thinks it important for Sue to hear it directly from her mother.)

MRS. ALLEN *(angrily): She could never believe that I was really sick. She thought that I was faking. It's hard for her to accept that I'll never get well. There is no cure for arthritis of the spine, you know. She would like me to get a full-time job, go out everyday, and never be sick.*

WORKER: *She's disappointed that you are not doing more.*

MRS. ALLEN: *Yes! Hell, I'd like to do more. I'd like to hold a job and get out.*

WORKER: *I guess you're a little disappointed in yourself.* (Worker skillfully helps Mrs. Allen acknowledge her own insecurity.)

MRS. ALLEN: *Very! But I can't do anything about it—just like my mother can't do anything about her illnesses. Lots of days she stays home because she doesn't feel well. Then she complains that we don't spend time with her.* (Evidence that the worker has touched on a sensitive point is provided in Mrs. Allen's fearful and vulnerable expression and her shifting to a "safer" subject, her mother. What she reveals, however, is the similarity between her behavior and her mother's behavior.)

WORKER: *She feels a little neglected.*

MRS. ALLEN: *Yes, and I can understand it because sometimes I feel like stopping Sue from going out. I'd like to say to her, "Please don't go."*

SUE: *I'd go anyway!*

MRS. ALLEN: *That's the wrong attitude.*

SUE: *It's not the wrong attitude.*

MRS. ALLEN   *(firmly): It's wrong because you should ask why I sometimes wish you'd stay home with me.*

WORKER: *You seem to be feeling a little neglected and alone yourself.*

MRS. ALLEN: *Uh-huh, I feel that a lot. I feel depressed a lot. I cry a lot. . . .*

SUE   *(interrupting): That's because she has problems.* (Sue addresses the worker, rather than her mother, possibly wanting to reaffirm that the worker's main concern is Sue.)

WORKER: *You mean your mother's physical problems?*

SUE: *No, she has mental problems, too. She has problems from way back that would take a long time and a lot of help to get her out of her depression and crying spells. When she's crying at home, I don't even want to be there. I'm not going to sit there being depressed because I know what she's crying about. And the things she cries about have been my problems for a long time. I'm going to try to get out. I'm not going to be depressed!*

WORKER: *What is your mother crying about?* (Worker feels that a family fear needs to be confronted: that the reasons for Mrs. Allen's depression were so traumatic that there was nothing anyone could do to help.)

SUE   *(after a pause): Death in the family, my father . . .*

MRS. ALLEN   *(interrupting defensively): My husband, my father, my brother. It's normal!*

SUE   *(yelling): It's not normal for ten years!*

MRS. ALLEN: *I went through it alone.*

WORKER: *That must have made it seem twice as long and difficult.*

Sue and Mrs. Allen then fell silent and exchanged looks expressing fear and anger.

WORKER   *(addressing Mrs. Allen): I think you deserve better. You don't need to endure mental pain on top of physical pain. You* deserve to be able to work through this. (Worker conveys her belief that there is something that can be done, thereby offering hope directly to Mrs. Allen and indirectly to Sue.)

MRS. ALLEN: *Well, I am more active now than I used to be.*

SUE: *Yes, but there's always coming home, and back to bed and back to memories.*

MRS. ALLEN: *It really isn't so bad as it was a couple of years ago because some of my friends have helped a lot.*

WORKER: *I'm sure that's true. But you have another option, you know. You can talk to someone professionally, just you alone.*

SUE: *I wish you would. It would help all of us.*

MRS. ALLEN: *These family sessions have been so helpful.*

SUE: *Sure, we get a better understanding of each other. But it still doesn't deal with what you've been feeling inside. I don't know what you've gone through in the past.* (Sue recognizes her mother's resistance and denial. At the same time, she sounds sympathetic.)

MRS. ALLEN: *I think it's silly to start reliving the past.*

SUE   *(angrily): You are anyway.*

MRS. ALLEN: *No, I'm getting over it. I'm not so bad as I was twelve years ago. Anyway, I didn't know of this option back then.*

WORKER   *(gently): Well, it's something you can think about now.*

MRS. ALLEN   *(slowly): Maybe I'll start thinking about it.*

WORKER: *Your daughter is really showing you how concerned she is.* (Worker offers a new interpretation of Sue's anger.)

SUE: *And I'm not going to be around forever. So you need to get yourself together.*

WORKER: *It sounds as if your daughter loves you enough to want what's best for you. And the best may mean getting yourself to feel better by talking to someone professionally.*

MRS. ALLEN   *(hesitantly): I know. I've been thinking about it. It's just hard to get up the energy.*

SUE: *I'll help you.*

In this interview, it was striking how consistently the worker's activity was directed toward Sue's key problem—her relationship with her mother. She enabled both Sue and Mrs. Allen to move away from their angry isolation and toward the expression of hope that a more positive relationship could be achieved.

The final interview with Sue took place nine months later. During the intervening months, the worker helped Sue clarify the limited extent of her responsibilities to her mother and grandmother, which enabled her to invest more energy in her school work and peer relationships. She slowly learned that she could disengage herself from her mother in a healthy way, without the guilt she had once felt. She graduated from high school and was preparing to start secretarial school in the fall. Mrs. Allen began to make a life of her own by obtaining a job. Both Sue and the worker agreed that Sue was ready to be independent of therapy as she began her adult life.

WORKER   *(as Sue comes into the interviewing room): You're smiling. What does that mean?*
SUE: *I just picked up our tickets for Florida and I'm getting really excited.*

Sue was to vacation with her boyfriend, Jerry, the following month, and she and the worker discussed the details of the trip briefly.

WORKER: *How is your mother taking all this?* (Worker goes back to the fundamental issue of the relationship with Sue's mother.)
SUE: *Some days she's fine and other days she rants and raves like a baby. I just don't listen to it anymore. I have to be responsible for me!* (Sue demonstrates the results of skilled counseling. She has developed a healthier sense of an independent self.)
WORKER: *What do you mean?* (Worker asks this question to stimulate Sue to recognize the gains she has made and thereby reinforce her new confidence and the lessening of guilt.)
SUE: *I'm not exactly sure. But I do know I can't live my life worrying about how my mother is going to react; if she's going to be sick and make me feel guilty. I know she doesn't like to have me and Jerry go to Florida together, but I have to do it— it's good for us.*
WORKER: *What does your mother object to?*
SUE: *She says it's because it's not right for us to travel together when we're not married. I know that's not it. It's because she doesn't want me to leave her.*
WORKER: *You sound sad about that.* (In responding to Sue's tone of voice rather than her spoken words, the worker acknowledges the dependency with which Sue is still struggling.)
SUE: *I am! All my life I felt so guilty every time I walked out of the house. Now that I'm really doing it without guilt, it's harder than I thought.*
WORKER: *There was a time some months back when you would have been angry at your mother.* (An important element of a

final interview is helping the client review the progress made, which the worker does in this comment.)

SUE: *Yes, I know, but I'm past that now. You know that.*

WORKER: *Yes I do, we both do. You have made changes, haven't you—like letting go of some of your anger? But at times like this, we wonder what to replace it with.*

SUE: *Yes, now that I don't feel so angry anymore. I just feel that I have to move on—make my own life.*

WORKER: *Any guilt with that?*

SUE: *A little—but not enough to make me stay.*

WORKER: *Why do you think that is?* (Worker senses that this is an important point that has to be clarified.)

SUE *(slowly): I guess because for once in my life I really feel that I deserve this.*

WORKER: *Yes, I think you do. But with the freedom comes the responsibility of making the decision that is right for you.* (Worker reinforces the assumption of the status of adulthood by point out the other side of the coin.)

SUE *(after a pause): You know, it's sort of half scary and half not.*

WORKER: *What do you mean?*

SUE: *Well, I know this is just the first test, going to Florida. After that it will be college and then getting married and all those kinds of things.*

WORKER: *What do all those kinds of things have in common?* (Worker is still pushing Sue to be fully aware of her feelings and the adjustments that will have to be made.)

SUE: *What do you mean?*

WORKER: *Well, you said Florida was the first test. A test of what?*

SUE: *I guess breaking away from my mother.*

WORKER: *Why is "breaking away" so important to you?* (Worker raises this question because it is important for Sue to recognize that separation can occur in a healthy way without guilt.)

SUE: *I know that when I used to stay in just because she made me feel guilty, I would be so angry. Now I can leave more easily because I know she has to be responsible for herself, and I don't feel so guilty or angry.*

WORKER: *Do you think your mother is aware of these changes?*

SUE: *Yes, after our meetings here, and she's been changing herself a little, too.*

WORKER: *What kind of changes do you see in her?*

SUE: *Well, she really is more independent—she got a job, you know. And she doesn't act so nosey about everything I do.*

WORKER: *Sounds as if everyday life has been a little easier.*

SUE: Yes, and I think my mother is happier too, now, even though
      she doesn't get any professional help as you suggested. It's al-
      most as if she's not ready yet, that she has to do some things for
      herself first.

WORKER: I think you're right. Everyone has her own way of deal-
      ing with things.

SUE: I don't think she was ready to talk to someone alone as I was
      with you. But I wish she was because I know how helpful it can
      be. (Sue affirms her recognition of the progress she has made in
      counseling—one more indication she is ready to be on her
      own.)

WORKER: You looked sad saying that.

SUE: Well, I am in a way, and I don't know why.

WORKER (after a few moments of silence): I wonder if you have
      some mixed feelings about our ending. (Worker encourages
      verbalization of the inevitable ambivalence clients feel at the
      point of termination, especially when a strong worker-client re-
      lationship has been developed.)

SUE (hesitating): Yes, maybe.

WORKER: You were saying how helpful our talks were, but you
      were looking sad, and I wonder if you don't feel that way,
      too—happy and sad at the same time?

SUE: I'm glad because I really feel I've changed for the better and
      things are better at home. But I'm sad because I don't know
      how I'm going to feel once I walk out of here. I was thinking
      about this before I came today and I almost didn't come.

WORKER: Then it must have taken a lot of strength to come.

SUE: Yes, because I knew I had to—that it wasn't going to be so
      bad.

WORKER: That you weren't going to feel guilty this time for leav-
      ing. (Worker finishes what she assumed was Sue's thought. This
      is usually not done but is permissible at the point of termination
      when the worker was quite sure of the accuracy of her
      interpretation.)

SUE: Yes, I guess that's it.

WORKER: Well, it's pretty natural and normal to have those mixed
      feelings, but you showed some real strength by allowing your-
      self to realize them. I think it's one of the most important
      things you could do. And one of those realizations was the fact
      that you don't have to feel guilty each time you leave someone.
      (The counseling contact is brought to a close with one final
      reference to the issue of guilt, which was Sue's central
      problem.)

SUE: *You're right, and I don't feel guilty because I think it's right for me.*

WORKER: *So do I think it's right for you.*

The interview ended with a little talk about Sue's future plans for school. Sue was encouraged to feel free to call the worker in the future if she had any special concerns.

21 "Don't tell me anymore what's wrong with me"

Rectifying an error and regaining a client's trust

The responsibility of social workers to elicit as fully as possible client participation in planning to solve or ameliorate their problems is a basic principle of professional practice. Sometimes, however, it happens that, for a variety of reasons, this principle is overlooked. A worker may unconsciously respond to subtle pressure, or manipulation from a family member, to bypass the client. The planning then proceeds without the knowledge and involvement of the client. Or a worker may become so anxious about discussing a plan that he knows or anticipates will be objectionable to the client that he cannot do so. The worker's wish, and need, to avoid a painful or controversial discussion can lead to failure to assure a client of his right to know and to plan, not to be "planned for" by others.

The following interview illustrates how a worker rectified her error when she became aware of how she had violated a basic, ethical principle of social work practice. For beginning interviewers, who, quite naturally, are concerned about "making mistakes," it is reassuring to know that they usually can repair any possible damage. Most clients who sense a worker's sincere interest and wish to help will respond to an honest admission of error or misjudgment, or the withholding of information that the client should have been given. In the case of Mrs. Dorothy Johnston, an independent, reserved woman, the worker came to realize the effect of withholding information about a plan for her care after discharge in time to preserve their relationship, and regain Mrs. Johnston's trust. As a result of the worker's facing up to her negligence, the interview resulted in a most poignant revelation of a universal need deeply felt by Mrs. Johnston.

During a hospital stay the previous autumn, Mrs. Johnston had been referred to the worker for help in planning home care after discharge. Living with her were an unmarried daughter, Adele, and her two teenage children, and another grandchild, Jean, eight years of age, whose mother, the youngest daughter of Mrs. Johnston, had died several years ago. Adele had moved into her mother's home about a year ago to help care for her. There were another unmarried daughter and son who lived in distant cities and maintained little contact with their mother.

Mrs. Johnston's income consisted of Social Security payments and foster care payments for Jean. Adele, who had given up her previous job, was enrolled in a vocational school training program for which she received a stipend.

The worker had occasional contacts when Mrs. Johnston attended clinic for follow-up care after surgery for cancer. She was aware of a strained relationship between Adele and her mother and maintained a telephone contact with the latter to be available if she needed further service.

Although her prognosis on discharge had been poor, Mrs. Johnston functioned well until shortly before readmission in early spring. Her condition was very serious: her diabetic condition was out of control, she had pneumonia with a high fever, and was unable to retain food. The worker was shocked at the drastic change in her—she showed a great loss of weight and general deterioration. The worker saw Mrs. Johnston and her daughter regularly and put plans in motion for home care. Mrs. Johnston underwent surgery twice to remove abscesses in a lung and the intestinal tract and her condition stabilized. The medical staff recommended transfer to a hospital where she would have twenty-four-hour supervision. Although ambivalent about this plan, and unwilling to have it presented to her mother, Adele, after friends spoke favorably of the chronic care hospital, agreed to follow through on an application. When the application was accepted, she agreed to keep the appointment for a preadmission interview, but still expressed the hope that "my mother will get well enough to come home."

There were marked changes in Mrs. Johnston's personality and behavior during this hospitalization. At the same time, Mrs. Johnston denied the seriousness of her condition and resisted verbalizing any feelings about it.

I interviewed Mrs. Johnston today to talk about discharge plans. I wanted to inform her about what was in process concerning home care services and to tell her about the application to Good Samaritan Hospital, of which she had not been informed. In light of the patient's condition the first few weeks after admission, it was not completely inappropriate to hold back on discussing the Good Samaritan application. However, as she improved and became alert again, her daughter and I should have involved her in the planning. Unfortunately, we did not and Mrs. Johnston became suspicious. In contrast to her usual nature, she became irritable and angry, first toward the nurses, then toward her daughter, and finally toward me. I felt that part of the cause of this behavior was the stage of her illness, but also because she was becoming increasingly isolated. Her anger brought about the realization, on my part, of what was going on and I talked to her daughter about involving her mother in the planning. Because of long-standing patterns of dysfunctional communication and a poor relationship with her mother, the daughter did not feel she could talk to her mother about it and asked me to do so.

I told Mrs. Johnston that I needed to talk with her about what had been happening concerning her discharge plans. I told her I was still in the process of obtaining home services for her, as she was aware. I said that there was something else we had been doing, something that I had not discussed with her before, but would like to do so now. I explained that even though she had been improving, she still required a lot of care. In trying to obtain that care, the doctors had recommended another hospital. Mrs. Johnston was a little unsettled by this and interrupted to ask why she needed another hospital—she was already in a hospital and she wanted to go home. I said I could understand that, but it would be a different kind of hospital. I told her it was Good Samaritan, a special hospital for cancer patients. She said that she didn't care what kind of hospital it was—she just wanted to go home. She didn't want to hear anymore about what was wrong with her; she knew her condition. She had gotten better and felt she was able to go home now, if she had some help. No doctor could make her go anywhere. It was up to her to decide. She continued to talk about her wishes and expressed anger that anyone would try to tell her what to do. I responded that she was right, no one had the right to tell her, or make her do anything, and we had been wrong to move in this direction without talking to her first. She continued to ventilate along these lines, expressing legitimate feelings of exclusion.

I explained that we considered the possibility only because of the amount of care she still needed at this time, and were concerned that it might not be enough at home. She said she knew it would not be as it was before, but with help, she thought she would be able to manage. She talked about how important it was for her to go home; she had to be with her grandchildren again. I responded that I could see how important it was for her and that I was sorry I had not been completely honest with her before. She said it was all right, I had told her now and that was the most important thing. Besides, she said, it wasn't all my fault, she was partly to blame, too, because she had not always been completely honest with me. Mrs. Johnston continued, saying she knew I had always been faithful to her, ever since she had been in the hospital the last time. She said even after she had left the hospital I had helped with the electric company when it threatened to cut off service and with her bus fares. And I had frequently called to see how she was feeling. She appreciated that very much. But there were things about her situation she had not been able to talk to anyone about before. She was going to write it all down in a book before she died. She would write a book. I responded that she had so much she wanted to say. Yes, she said, there was a lot in her life she wanted to say. She wanted me to understand why she had to go home. Her grandchildren were there and she had to be with them, especially little Jean. She stopped talking and began to cry. We were sitting close, opposite one another, and I reached out and held her hand. Mrs. Johnston had always been reserved and reluctant to talk about her feelings. I felt she desperately wanted to. She had a lot built up inside her, but it was hard for her.

She continued to talk, crying as she did. She said those grandchildren meant everything to her. She wanted them to be raised right. She thought she had done the best she could with her own children, but they were no good. She tried to hide it and pretend they were good, but they weren't. And she was so ashamed, so embarrassed. She felt so guilty about it, wondering what she had done wrong. She told me a few instances where she felt her daughters had treated her badly and acted immorally with men. In a few moments, she began to calm down and said she was glad she had explained her situation to me. Now, I could see how important it was for her to go home—she would not go to another hospital. I responded that I could see how important it was to her, how much her grandchildren meant to her and how some of the things her children had done hurt her. Mrs. Johnston smiled and said I was going to be in her book too. I smiled back and said her book seemed like a good way for her to say a lot of things she wanted to *say but had never been able to do before. Yes, she replied, things she had just explained to me. I said that we could keep talking about the things she wanted to put in her book.*

She asked me if I would come to visit her when she left the hospital; she would like me to come to her house when she got home. I told Mrs. Johnston that I didn't think I could do that. (As hard as it was for me to say this, I knew I could not make a promise I could not keep, especially because I would be leaving the hospital. If I had not been leaving, I probably would have said yes, and made a home visit. As it turns out, I'm glad I had to say no, so that we were able to get at what was behind the request.) Mrs. Johnston started to cry again and said she just didn't want me to forget her. She never wanted me to forget her after she died. I told Mrs. Johnston that she was a very special person to me and I would never forget her. We sat for a few more moments and she said she was glad we had talked because she felt better now. She added that she wanted to go back to her room. I thanked her for sharing with me all that she had and kissed her as I got up to leave. She smiled and I told her I would be back to see her that afternoon.

After the interview, the worker made this assessment of it:

I feel that Mrs. Johnston was finally able to talk about some of her feelings. It was difficult for her to do so. She told me that she was brought up to mind her own business and keep it to herself. The book she spoke of writing can be used metaphorically to help her talk. Mrs. Johnston seemed to be trying to come to terms with herself, she was reliving parts of her life, wondering what she could have done differently. She was questioning a lot—the part she played in raising her children, what went wrong or where she had failed so that they became "no-good" or maybe not what she had hoped they would be.

When Mrs. Johnston said she did not want me to forget her after she died, she was saying a lot. She put this on a personal level toward me. I felt she was reaching for a personal contact and I responded on that level. But I think she was saying more. Although she did refer specifically to me in this instance, she probably extended her wish to be remembered in general as well. I did not address this, perhaps, in addition to my comment, I could have said that she wanted to be remembered, or something to acknowledge this desire. The book is also something she could leave behind to be remembered by.

When the worker informs Mrs. Johnston of the recommendation for continued hospital care elsewhere, she becomes upset and questions the need, and expresses her desire to return home. She minimizes her condition and angrily affirms her right to make her own decisions. The worker accepts her anger and admits that she and the daughter had been wrong to proceed without consulting Mrs. Johnston. She explains the amount of care Mrs. Johnston needs, and the latter, repeating her wish to go home, begins to explain why it is important for her to be there. When the worker apologizes for not having been honest with her, Mrs. Johnston accepts the apology and reveals that she, too, has withheld some information from the worker. Mrs. Johnston says that the worker has been trustworthy in the past and has been helpful and concerned. This positive acceptance of the worker's apology is possible because of the relationship established during and after Mrs. Johnston's previous hospitalization. Mrs. Johnston, although angry, does not forget how faithful the worker has been to her.

Mrs. Johnston's feelings come through: her failure as a mother, her strong wish to do better for her grandchildren than she seemed to do in raising her children, and finally, the universal need of persons facing the prospect of death to be remembered. She fantasizes writing a book to explain her life and the feelings she finds so hard to express. She reaches out to the worker for assurance that she will not be forgotten and the worker responds with a personal expression of affection. Aware of how much this reserved woman has revealed in this emotionally charged interview, the worker tells her that she will come to see her later in the day—a reassurance that she is indeed a "special person" whom the worker will not forget.

22 "I figured, out of sight, out of mind"

Counseling for problems affecting job performance

In chapter 12, reference was made to the development of counseling programs for employees of some organizations and for members of some unions. The employing organization may provide counseling for its employees in a special department within the organization or it may contract with a family service agency to pay for counseling services. The case in this chapter is illustrative of the latter arrangement

Although many employees may be relieved to have recognition of and help with their personal or job problems by their employers, others may be greatly concerned, and suspicious that damaging information will be reported to their employers and result in loss of jobs. In some employer programs established to counsel alcoholics, supervisors are instructed to warn the employee that his job is indeed in jeopardy if he does not accept and act on a referral for professional help. In the following case, no such threat had been made. The client had applied on his own initiative to the employee assistance program of a local family service agency. Even so, he was extremely concerned about the confidentiality of the interview.

The employee, Tom Barrett, was a thirty-one-year-old salesman with six years' experience in his current job. He had been recently divorced, and had no children. Previously, he had been one of the top salesmen in his field but had not closed a sale in the last four months.

During the initial interview, he stated that his health was poor and that his doctor had told him he drank too much. He acknowl-

164

edged that he drank too much, but said it was because of the stress he experienced at work. He claimed that he was being persecuted for a personal reason and had been removed from lucrative accounts by a vindictive district sales manager. He was vague about what the personal reason might be, but felt his job was in jeopardy.

As the interview progressed, it was apparent that Mr. Barrett had a pattern of alcoholism that was interfering with his ability to work. He denied it, but said he was willing to go for treatment to get a break from the job. His denial in the face of overwhelming evidence, including blackouts and liver malfunction, was typical of alcoholics even as they are admitted for treatment. He also revealed that he took various drugs.

The interview presented below was conducted two days after Mr. Barrett completed a twenty-eight-day stay at an alcoholic rehabilitation center where he had been referred by the counselor. The interview began with his describing his experiences at the rehabilitation center. His reaction to the stay there was positive, although the staff had found him a difficult patient and in telephone conferences with the counselor had questioned whether he was sufficiently motivated to benefit or whether he just "wanted a vacation." The recording starts where the counselor begins to ask about his job.

COUNSELOR: *That was the point when your drinking got totally out of hand?*

MR. BARRETT: *It got totally insane.*

COUNSELOR: *So you had two points where—one—where they took the first major account away?*

MR. BARRETT: *Right.*

COUNSELOR: *And that's where you started to really hit it bad and continued to hit it bad.*

MR. BARRETT: *Until January 1st.*

COUNSELOR: *Until January 1st?*

MR. BARRETT: *Until January 1st, because we had another change in management and I was working for someone who was on my side.*

COUNSELOR: *They looked at your record and they said, "What's going on here? How did we lose this customer?"*

MR. BARRETT: *And then they said, "Look, let's get him back," and Miss Lawrence, my boss, made an action plan which was attainable and I was working very hard toward it. But, all of a sudden, they pulled out the rugs from both of us. In addition to*

affecting my performance, it affected my boss in her perfor-
mance. It affected everything in a negative manner, and it
started, you know, from purely lousy, personal reasons.

COUNSELOR: *That may or may not be true, but the question is*
what is going to happen when you get back to work? (Counselor asks a concrete question to focus client's attention on the
reality of his return to work, rather than continue his discussion
of "the lousy, personal reasons" which may not exist.)

MR. BARRETT: *Well, when I go back to work, the issue is still not*
resolved and this last situation that they created by removing
my accounts and scoring out my action plan—I reported that
incident to Personnel with documentation. Personnel is very
concerned about how the field is being managed, and when I go
back, the issue is going to be reopened, because they have to
know why it was done from the management point and they
want to know what they're going to do to correct the situation.

COUNSELOR: *So when you get back you're going to be in the mid-*
dle of a controversy.

MR. BARRETT: *Yes, absolutely. I have to be in the middle of a*
controversy.

COUNSELOR: *It's okay. I'm not saying you should or shouldn't be,*
but you're still going to be hot. You're still going to be a person
who is going to be identified as a troublemaker, or as a person
who will be seen by some people as making trouble. (Counselor
again affirms the reality the client will have to face on his job.)

MR. BARRETT: *Right, but when I go back, I'll go back with a clear*
mind knowing that taking alcohol and taking drugs aren't going
to fix the problem.

COUNSELOR: *I asked you how you thought the alcohol and in-*
creased drug taking affected your behavior after June, but you
skipped right over to January 1st, and I'm wondering if you
know what happened to you . . . what you were doing? (Counselor points out how client has evaded discussing the effects of
his addictions and seeks to ascertain if he is aware of what happened to him during a six-month period.)

MR. BARRETT: *Yes, I know what happened. I'm pretty careful and*
I try not to drink in the office; I don't want people seeing me
get sloshed in the office. Like every other office, there are cer-
tain people you become personal friends with, who are aware
of what's going on, and particularly in a sales organization,
everybody knows when someone's getting screwed, and most
sales people are very sympathetic to other sales people, be-
cause if it can happen to one person it can happen to another.

So occasionally, I would go out and have a couple of drinks with people in the office but I would try to be careful to the point where I wouldn't want to have anything repeated and I really didn't let everything out. And if I was going to do any real bitching, I'd do it by myself away from the office where people weren't in a position to repeat something or to go back and say "Wow! This guy's got a terrible attitude." So, self-preservation is always there, and self-preservation is probably what brought me into this ridiculous situation now. (Client's response is vague and rambling, ending with a confused statement about "self-preservation.")

COUNSELOR: *I don't have a clear idea. Maybe it's because you don't have a clear idea about how it was that your behavior on the job and your relationship to people on the job changed— how they changed, not why but how they changed when you increased your drinking.* (A nonaccusatory comment to help client think more clearly.)

MR. BARRETT: *Some of the people whom I drink with on the job probably drink more than I do, a whole lot more, so my behavior to them has not changed at all. Nondrinkers I didn't have much to do with simply because in my particular job you don't have to go into the office every day. The only time you really had to spend in the office was when you were giving a presentation in your own facility or if you had to go in and do a report, or something like that. Everybody sort of works for himself almost. So you will have a two-minute conversation. "How are you?" or "What's going on?" and that's it. I don't really think people are aware of what my problems are, and by the same token, I am not aware of what's going on in their territories or lives.* (Client continues to ramble.)

COUNSELOR: *Was there a change in how you were with the customers?* (Again, the counselor uses a question to elicit specific information.)

MR. BARRETT: *No, I have always dealt with the customers pretty much the same, because you have to, because the customers pay my salary. So I didn't go into the office and I was staying home. What I would do is handle whatever business I had from my home just as I would be doing it at the office.* (Client continuing to evade giving any information which could reflect negatively on his job performance.)

COUNSELOR: *You mean over the telephone?*

MR. BARRETT: *Yes, over the phone. "What's the trouble?" "How can I help you?" "Let's make an appointment." When you're a commission salesman, what you actually have is a desk and a telephone. That's your business right there, and the size of your desk or the color of your telephone does not make you success- ful or not successful. In my instance, I just used the telephone in my house, simply because I didn't feel like seeing anyone in the office, then I can get more work done and there's more privacy.*

COUNSELOR: *So you were avoiding going into work?* (The con- crete question "cuts through" the client's rationalization.)

MR. BARRETT: *Yes.*

COUNSELOR: *And that was different?*

MR. BARRETT: *Excuse me?*

COUNSELOR: *That's different from what you were doing before?*

MR. BARRETT: *I'm a little bit lost on that one.* (Client claims not to understand a simple, clear statement; perhaps he is "stall- ing" for time to think how best to respond.)

COUNSELOR: *I asked you how things were different, and you said that for the last three or four months, rather than go in, since all you needed was the telephone to contact people, you would work at home, so that you could avoid running into people at work.* (Counselor does not question his "being lost," but calmly repeats an explanation of his question.)

MR. BARRETT: *Yes.*

COUNSELOR: *Now, that's a change from what you were doing two years ago.* (When the client answers affirmatively, the coun- selor continues to emphasize the fact that the client avoids going to his office.)

MR. BARRETT: *Well, two years ago I used to go into the office.*

COUNSELOR: *So, there was a change?*

MR. BARRETT: *Yes.*

COUNSELOR: *So, you wouldn't go in because you didn't want to encounter anyone there?*

MR. BARRETT: *Yes. I figured, out of sight, out of mind.*

COUNSELOR: *What would be out of your mind if you didn't see them?*

MR. BARRETT: *Well, if I'm out of sight, I'm out of their mind.*

COUNSELOR: *What would they think if they saw you? You were avoiding something. You're running this past me as if to say, "Well, you know, this thing happened because somebody six- teen levels above me wanted to help out his buddy." But mean- while, something was actually happening with you, too.*

MR. BARRETT: *Let me put it this way. In a sales organization, most of the time, management will tell you, "What the hell are*

you doing in the office? You are supposed to be in the field."
And the situation I was in, I had done a little bit of bitching
and moaning about the way they handled my accounts. (In
these exchanges, the client discusses his behavior and the problems he experienced—or anticipated might happen on the
job—always projecting responsibility on to "the management."
He reveals feelings of vulnerability related to his thinking that
management is overly critical or inherently hostile to its sales
personnel.)

COUNSELOR: *Yes.*

MR. BARRETT: *In fact, the account was even concerned about it
and sent a letter saying that they thought I should be put back,
but the way I handled it, I didn't want to give management an
opportunity to do something funny.*

COUNSELOR: *Whom do you mean when you say management?*

MR. BARRETT: *Management would be the next level higher than
my immediate boss.*

COUNSELOR: *So, you have your sales manager.*

MR. BARRETT: *I have no problem with her.*

COUNSELOR: *And your district manager.*

MR. BARRETT: *I had a problem with him.*

COUNSELOR: *Whom you were avoiding?*

MR. BARRETT: *Correct.*

COUNSELOR: *What would happen when you would see that
person?*

MR. BARRETT: *Nothing.*

COUNSELOR: *Then what were you avoiding?*

MR. BARRETT: *I didn't want to be put in a position where someone would say, "What the hell are you doing in the office instead of being in the field?"*

COUNSELOR: *That had been said to you?*

MR. BARRETT: *No, it had not been said to me, but I just wanted
to avoid that particular person, because I didn't trust him and I
didn't want to give him any opportunity to say, "What are you
doing in the office? Let me see your plan. What have you done
today? What have you got for tomorrow?" I simply wanted to
avoid him because it was not nice seeing him because there's
bad feeling and he can always say, "You are spending too much
time in the office," or, "You're not doing this or you're not
doing that." In a sales organization, as long as you're doing
your job and bringing in business, then they really don't care
what you are doing. And my intention was to make money as
best I can, with the least amount of hassle. And seeing this*

person and getting hassled consistently would affect my income.

COUNSELOR: *How?*

MR. BARRETT: *How? How? Because they could—they could— they could put you on. How? If you are in a sales organization, you know you have to work and get compensated for it. If someone's always busting your horns, it puts you under a cer- tain amount of pressure and you just get fed up with it and you don't do the job that you should be doing. Whereas, if you could avoid the hassle you could do a better job.*

COUNSELOR: *When you get fed up and this man is "busting your horns," what happens to you that makes it harder for you to work? What happens when you experience this tension be- tween you and the other man that interferes with your work?*

MR. BARRETT: *What happens to me is that I have to spend more time planning how to avoid this person. Another way of saying it is that I would have to spend more time planning to protect myself as opposed to going out and securing more business. I would have to spend more time writing silly memos just to cover myself—I would have to spend more time documenting the most insignificant factor of the day.*

COUNSELOR: *You would feel exposed.*

MR. BARRETT: *Yes, yes, you have to cover yourself.*

COUNSELOR: *You mean you would feel vulnerable.*

MR. BARRETT: *Sure, and the only thing I used to do is spend "x" amount of time trying to cover myself via memo, and if some- one said, "What are you doing in the office?" I would say, "Well, I'm writing this memo in response to something that was mentioned yesterday and in addition I have copied in so-and-so and so-and-so." That way, if someone says, "What were you doing in the office on a certain day at 2 o'clock in the after- noon?" I can say I was responding to a memo, and just to make sure that there was no mistake, I wanted to put what I was doing in writing. And I got to a point where I spent more time trying to protect myself—very valuable time if you are a com- missioned salesman, because you are much better off in front of customers. It was just a matter of self-preservation.*

COUNSELOR: *You're hoping that it's going to be different now.*

MR. BARRETT: *I am absolutely certain that it is going to be different.*

COUNSELOR: *How do you think you will be able to make it dif- ferent when you get back?*

MR. BARRETT: *Sell. I think the difference has already been made because they messed up too bad the first time around.*

COUNSELOR: *What is it that you're going to do? I understand that you think that it's something that they did which put some pressure on you, and you dealt with that according to the procedures. But you're going to go back and you're still going to walk into that place and see a lot of familiar faces.*

MR. BARRETT: *When I go back in, the one thing that has not been resolved is the action plan, which, in fact, has to be addressed by Personnel.*

COUNSELOR: *This is the plan that sets out goals and targets for you that you should be doing at a certain time?*

MR. BARRETT: *Correct.*

COUNSELOR: *And you had worked that out with your supervisor a couple of months ago?*

MR. BARRETT: *Correct, so I have to sit down and make a new plan. When I come back, the old situation is still there and has to be resolved because I brought it to management's attention. They will also be involved in writing out the plan.*

COUNSELOR: *So you have to do a revised and updated plan.*

MR. BARRETT: *Correct, which I think is good. And they also have to address the old issue of policy. They have to straighten that out.* (When asked to explain his certainty that he can effect a different situation on returning to the job, the client expresses grandiose plans and ideas.)

COUNSELOR: *Okay. Let's try to break it down by a time schedule.*

MR. BARRETT: *Within the first week, I will have to meet with my immediate manager, who will sit down and we will fill out the plan. I follow out the plan to the best of my ability and I may have to ask for additional training on hardware because I have not touched the hardware within the last couple of months. I may have to spend two or three days learning hardware so that I can demonstrate it properly. I will probably have to do a lot of reading to become more aware, and then I will have to look at the territory I am going back into, figure it out both geographically and where the opportunities are. I will have to contact all the people in my territory and give demonstrations and presentations, and follow through to the point of closing the order. I am very prepared to do it, because one thing about selling is that it is a very basic occupation. There are certain steps and procedures that have to be followed to get an order. That's the only way you can survive. It is almost like a science.*

It's like a disease. There are symptoms when someone is going to buy. There are steps they are going to go through before they are going to buy and there are decisions they are going to have to make. You just lead them down the garden path. You have to keep a very big prospect list because customers are human and things happen. They may not get budget approval in a certain amount of time, so you always have to keep an active prospect list.

COUNSELOR: *Do you see any reason, from your point of view, why your manager should be in touch with me? Why you would want your manager, who is working on your plan, to be in touch with me? Or, do you think we are better off keeping your contact here strictly confidential, where I have nothing to do with your office?* (Recognizing the grandiose thinking as a trait of early sobriety, the counselor does not challenge it. He focuses the rest of the interview on whether he is to have a contact with the client's supervisor, on supporting his client's respect for the one person he seems to trust, and on accepting the client's planning for their next appointment.)

MR. BARRETT: *My gut feeling is that I would like to keep our relationship separate until such time that I can speak with her, which will probably be within the next few days, and just figure out where she is. I would like to feel comfortable with where she is rather than open up a can of worms.*

COUNSELOR: *So, you still have to feel out what your new plan will look like because you're not sure what's happened in the past month?*

MR. BARRETT: *After I speak to her, I'll have some indication of how she feels about my being back on the team. If I feel that she's concerned, and I feel it's necessary, maybe I will ask her to give you a call.*

COUNSELOR: *Okay. So we'll leave that until after you've spoken to her. There are many things that would remain confidential.*

MR. BARRETT: *She's aware that I am an alcoholic and that I'm an addict. She came to visit me in the rehabilitation center, and she's a nice person. But the fact of the matter is, she's a new manager.*

COUNSELOR: *I guess she'll look good if you look good.*

MR. BARRETT: *And if I do bad she does bad. And what they've done is they've already knocked me down and, in effect, they've given her a pretty good punch.*

COUNSELOR: *So the two of you have mutual goals in some sense.*

MR. BARRETT: *Yes, and it's strictly if I do well, she does well. If* they're constantly on my back and taking accounts away from me, it affects her performance as well. She appears to be a nice person who is interested in doing a job. We are not personal friends, it's just that I respect her as a manager. She's bright and she's aware of the political situation. I wouldn't want to do anything to hurt her. She's been honest and she's been open, and the fact of the matter is that the decisions that were made affecting me were beyond her control. She did everything in her power to protect me. It's her immediate manager where the problem exists.

COUNSELOR: *So you're really helping her in a sense to deal with these pressures.*

MR. BARRETT: Yes. My being in here now certainly takes an awful lot of pressure off her and gives me an opportunity to get my health back in shape.

COUNSELOR: *When are you going to see your physician?*

MR. BARRETT: I have to go to an outpatient clinic tonight and go see my physician tomorrow. I think all I do is go to AA meetings and doctors.

COUNSELOR: *How are we going to leave this between the two of us? I'm available to see you.*

MR. BARRETT: I'll have to call you in a couple of days to make an appointment. Meanwhile, I want to check out some other rehab centers where I might be able to get some physical help because my body is shot. I've heard about another place and I'm going to talk to someone there. What I'd like to do is find another institution where I can get some extra therapy while it's available. So I'll call you and we'll arrange a time for next week.

COUNSELOR: *Fine.*

This interview illustrates some of the tasks and problems facing counselors in industrial social work. Establishing a helping relationship with Tom Barrett is more difficult because he defends himself by the denial, evasiveness, and projection of an alcoholic. The counselor was aware that his client, although he had applied to the agency voluntarily, apparently was motivated chiefly by a wish to gain the support and possible influence of the agency in his struggles with management. Prior to his coming to the agency, he had filed a grievance, stating that he was entitled to continue collecting a commission from an account that he had originally obtained, which he referred to in the interview as having been taken from him.

Despite the counselor's initial interpretation that he functioned independently from anyone in the client's organization, he is placed by the client in the middle of an adversary situation—a perception by the client which strongly influences the quality of the interview. The client continues to be very guarded and is careful not to reveal any unfavorable evidence about his job performance.

Furthermore, the normal suspiciousness of a client in an employer-financed program is increased by the fact that Mr. Barrett is in the very early stages of sobriety and his thinking is still fuzzy. The counselor correctly tries to be concrete in his questions and statements and he does, at times, help the client focus his discussion more realistically. Another important observation about this interview is that Mr. Barrett's remarks become vague or tangential whenever his relationship to other employees is touched on.

The client's stated motivation of self-preservation is accepted as indeed valid as the counselor stays with that theme by his focus on what Mr. Barrett needs to do to keep his job. However, two other aspects of early sobriety, the employee's underlying resentment of those in superior positions and his grandiose thinking of how he will function in the future, interfere with his ability to analyze his situation clearly. Whether he will succeed in keeping his job cannot be assumed.

The counselor sees the most important area of his help in this initial period as supporting Mr. Barrett's ability to stay sober. In the early portion of the interview, which has not been reported here, the focus was on his drinking and its negative effect on his ability to function. In the judgment of the counselor, helping his client maintain sobriety is the most important aspect of the contact at this time.

23 "My mother should never have got a divorce in the first place"

Treating a remarried family with adolescents

This case is the second illustration of counseling a remarried family. In contrast to the Mansfields, whose marriage was new, the Grants had been married for six years. The family interview demon· strates the greater complexity of the problems faced by the remarried family when there are adolescent children and when family members have not resolved relationship difficulties left over from the first marriage. This family situation also is a useful illustration of how the stepparent-stepchild relationship can complicate the achievement of the normal developmental tasks of adolescence.

The Grant family is composed of Jack Grant, aged forty-four years, Karen Grant, aged thirty-six years, and Mrs. Grant's two sons by her previous marriage to Bill Stuart, sixteen-year-old Peter and twelve-year-old Mark. Mrs. Grant made the application by phone to a family service agency at the suggestion of a friend who was also remarried and had received help. Mrs. Grant said that after some initial adjustment difficulties following her marriage to Mr. Grant, "things settled in." Now the family "is at the crossroads" and needs help. She accepted an appointment for the entire family.

After introducing her husband and the two boys, Mrs. Grant explained that this was the second marriage for her and the first for Mr. Grant. She and her first husband divorced after nine years of a stormy marriage when Peter was eight years of age and Mark was four. The boys saw their father only irregularly, but they seemed to accept this arrangement, which she welcomed because, even after the divorce, she and her former husband inevitably quarrel. About a year after her divorce, she met Jack Grant and they were married six months later. Mrs. Grant explained that there had been some very hard initial adjustments because Peter was very cold and indifferent toward her new husband. His behavior had come as a surprise, because Jack had spent a great deal of time with them as a family before she married and Peter had voiced no negative feelings about him. In time, however, Jack had won Peter over and they established a reasonably good relationship. In contrast, Mark immediately accepted his stepfather. Mrs. Grant said that the problem that brought them to the agency for therapy at this time was that Peter once again was unaccepting of his stepfather. He was rude and surly in his relationship to him and even at times to her, especially when she came to her husband's defense.

I suggested that it would be helpful to hear from each family member about his or her perception of the current difficulty and how each thought I could be of help.

Mr. Grant reaffirmed his wife's statement of the problem but added that it just might be a normal part of growing up. He was aware of the difficulties of this period of life from his own childhood experiences, and he did not want to magnify the problem if it were just a phase. On the other hand, if it was something serious, he did not want to ignore it. I stated that the teenage years are often difficult at best, but suggested that we explore together what behaviors were related to Peter's being in this phase and what behaviors were related to other factors that may explain the current difficulties.

I invited the boys to give their view of the situation. Peter said that he had nothing to say; he was there only because he was told he had to come. He felt that his parents should just leave him alone. When I queried Mark about his view of the situation, he said that he has no complaints and everything was fine as far as he was concerned. I commented that I knew it was hard to open up but that it was important for everyone to have a chance to say what he or she felt and to present his or her ideas of what was going on. I expressed the hope that as the interview progressed, Peter and Mark would feel free to agree or disagree and make their own wishes known about things in the family that they felt were some of the difficulties.

Mr. Grant encouraged the boys to speak out, asking, "How else can we get the help we need as a family?" He added that things are very uncomfortable for everyone now: "The house is like a cloud of gloom." He, for one, would like to see things return to the earlier climate of less tension. I empathized with the difficulty he was experiencing but asked if anything had happened that might help us understand the shift. After an uncomfortable silence of several minutes, Mark volunteered that there was a difference now. In an accusatory tone, he said that Peter had upset everything by contacting their father and having regular visits with him. For some years, neither he nor Peter had any contact with their father; they had put all their efforts into becoming part of their new family. Now, Peter was changing all of this by getting his father back into the picture. Mark added that everyone in the house was nervous about this, but no one talked openly about it.

I asked what there was about Peter's seeing his father that seemed to make everyone so nervous. For several minutes there was general shuffling of feet and avoidance of eye contact, each family member appearing to be waiting for the others to speak. Mrs. Grant finally spoke up, saying that Peter's seeing his father was tearing up the family. Things had gone smoothly until this new development—they had almost been able to forget that they were not the original family. Because Jack had no children, and her former husband was rarely involved with the two boys, it was as if they were no different from any other family. The boys had even used the Grant name in school. Now, with the boys' father back in the picture, Mrs. Grant found herself tense and nervous every time the telephone rang. If she picked up the phone and it was her ex-husband calling, she found herself arguing with him just as she had before the divorce. She did not know how to disentangle herself. She knew, however, that her upset state about this situation was one of the causes of the tension in the home.

At this point, Peter interjected, "My mother should never have got a divorce in the first place." He had always resented her decision and knew that his father had not wanted a divorce. He could not understand why everyone was so upset because he wanted to see his father! Mark, on the other hand, said that he did not understand why Peter could not let things alone, and why he had to stir things up by getting in touch with his father. As far as Mark was concerned, his father had abandoned him during the past few years when he never called or made any effort to see them. After some arguing between the boys about their differing perception of their father's role, Peter declared that he did not know why Mark couldn't feel the way he wanted to and he, Peter, have a right to feel the way he wanted. He went on to talk of his feeling that this right was denied him, not only by Mark, but by everyone else in the house. He felt as if he was fighting the entire family.

In an effort to clarify whether the coalition among family members that Peter described could be generalized to situations in addition to the current conflict about visits with the nonresident biological father, I asked Peter whether his feeling of being isolated from the rest of the family was also true for other things. After a long, thoughtful pause, Peter said that he had never really felt excluded by them until this issue came up. In fact, he would have described them as a very close family. Yet, he added, for about a year he had felt a great urge to have some contact with his father. In response to my encouragement to tell us more about this urge, he said that he felt that seeing his father was like learning more about himself. He had called his father on the spur of the moment when he remembered some of the nice things that they had done together before his parents got divorced. He also remembered how he enjoyed being with his father, and his feeling that he was always able to talk to him. When he had called, his father had been delighted and immediately offered to make arrangements for them to see each other.

(I thought that it was important to explore with Peter his feelings about the meaning of this contact with his father, and then to inquire into the anxieties his action stimulated in other members of the family. Clarifying the dynamics operating in this area would facilitate the clarification of family interactional patterns. It would also permit the examination of distortions and unrealistic apprehensions, and the exploration of realistic options.)

I asked Peter to talk a little about what it had meant to him to have reestablished contact with his father. He said that it really felt good to see his father. It made him feel good to have a view of his father that was different from the negative view held by his mother and his brother. No one had given his father a fair chance to be heard. His father had explained many things to him about why he had not insisted on visitation rights and about the relationship between himself and Peter's mother. Now, Peter understood things from his father's side as well as from his mother's. And in regard to his father's not seeing the boys during the period after his mother married, Peter said that his father had felt they should have a chance to work things out as a new family and he had not wanted to interfere. His father was sorry now that he had not visited them because it was so easy for his sons to see him as not caring, when he really always did care a lot.

The family became chaotic after Peter's remarks. Mrs. Grant grew very defensive about her decision to divorce her first husband,

and Mark and Mr. Grant came to her defense. She was also angry because Peter was idealizing his father and not remembering him as he really had been. I intervened in an effort to refocus the interview and to de-escalate the arguing by suggesting that the dissolution of any family by divorce was a difficult and painful event for all; it was understandable that there were differing perceptions about the validity of the decision. I also remarked that the decision in this instance had been made long ago and that perhaps we needed to refocus on the fact that the reasons for such a decision are not always clear to the children in the family, yet they have to live with it. I said it was not unusual for a child to be angry toward one or the other parent when he could not know what really happened. I suggested that we now consider where we could go from the present situation to help all the members of the family.

Mrs. Grant was the one to respond, saying that she and Jack had worked hard to be good parents to the children. She had been disappointed when Peter had not responded to Jack at first, but she had come to accept the fact that he and Jack might never have as close a relationship as Mark and Jack. The family had managed to work out a fairly comfortable pattern. She was not prepared for the rudeness and indifference that Peter was now displaying toward her husband. She found herself coming to her husband's defense and experiencing great anger toward Peter for upsetting the family. Peter said he did not understand why his mother had such a need to defend Jack. He thought that they could work things out between themselves if she would stay out of it. Mrs. Grant then used Peter's reference to "Jack" as evidence of the change in him since he had seen his father; before that happened, he had referred to his stepfather as "Dad." Peter denied it, and said it was his own idea; he was even thinking of going back to using his father's surname.

Mr. Grant said that this threat was what was upsetting the family. He added that in his head he knew the boys' father had a right to be with them. His hope had been, however, that over the years he and the boys would build a strong enough relationship so that they would not want to see their father. His goal had been to "be a father" to them. He had no children of his own, and he regarded Peter and Mark as his own sons. He talked for some time about how meaningful it was for him to have had a share in helping the boys grow up over the past few years. Peter then asked if his father hadn't always sent child support and wasn't that evidence that he also cared for them? Mr. Grant acknowledged that they had received regular child support payments, but added that it hardly paid

for all the things the boys needed: "I feel I really support you and
am more your real father than he has been."

Peter then said that Jack did not have to support him anymore;
he could always leave and live with his father. In an effort to de-
escalate the mounting tension and refocus the interview on realistic
alternatives, I remarked that the family balance had been upset by
the re-entry of the boys' father into the life of the family. I said I
was aware that this was difficult for all of them, but was suggesting
that we consider the various options open to them. Peter immediately declared that one option that was not available was for him
to stop seeing his father; which was what everyone else wanted. I
said I realized that the rest of the family seemed to be worried
about the changes in the family his continuing to see his father
might bring about. I suggested that perhaps we could talk about
what they feared might happen.

Mrs. Grant said that she wished Peter had not felt the need to
reach out to his father. Somehow, it made her feel that she was
responsible for hurting her former husband and taking something
away from him because of the divorce. Yet the marriage had not
been good and she really thought it would be better for the boys if
she got a divorce. She thought that if she could learn not to get
caught in the old resentments, maybe she could accept Peter's wanting to see his father. She knew that her ex-husband had a legal right
to see his children, and no court in the world would deny him that
right. It was just that "his phoning brings back so many unhappy
memories," and she found herself reverting to all of her old patterns. Mr. Grant said he had thought that that period of his wife's
life was finished, and he resented her being brought back into it.
Mark very quietly added, "It was bad enough having one family
break up."

I then stated that the feelings each of them had been expressing
were quite valid and I accepted them as real. I continued that I was
interested in Mr. Grant's earlier comments about normal developmental behavior in adolescence, and I thought that we might consider what he had said in relation to Peter's urge to see his father.
(My purpose in doing this was to help the family move from seeing
Peter's initiation of this contact as a rejection of them and a de-
preciation of the stepfather to seeing it as an expression of adolescent strivings for roots and for a sense of continuity as he worked on
the issues of identity and becoming a person in his own right.) I
stated that although this was an issue for any family with adolescent
children, it became more complicated in the remarried family be-

cause of the normal process of separation and establishing one's individual identity was often in conflict with the remarried family's goals of having all members tightly welded together in a close family unit. In addition, in this family there were fears that it would jeopardize the balance and security the new family had achieved. I said that perhaps there were alternative ways to view the situation and to deal with the change in the family picture. We needed to determine whether the threat they perceive was indeed avoidable. At this point, Peter interrupted with a remark that he didn't really want to leave home. He did appreciate everything that Jack had done for him. He realized that he had made threats when he was angry that he was not allowed to have feelings about his father that were not the same as the feelings of the others.

I commented on the complexity of family situations in which there was a nonresident parent who had the legal right to be involved with his or her children, when some family members were fearful that this would somehow jeopardize their family situation while others wanted to be involved with the nonresident parent. (My purpose was to defuse the scapegoating of Peter and to identify this as a family problem not only for the Grants but for remarried families in general.)

Closing the interview, I asked each of them to comment on what each one would like to work on and see as the outcome of the work with the agency. Mr. Grant said that he would like to feel more secure about his place with the boys and wanted his wife to be less agitated when her ex-husband called. Mrs. Grant said that she wanted to be less nervous about her former husband's phone calls. Mark said that he wanted things to be less tense, and Peter said that he wanted to have the right to see his father without hassles. I agreed that all of these goals were important and were really closely interrelated. I said that we would talk about these issues in the family session the following week.

No further commentary seems to be needed because the worker has so clearly recorded her reasons for conducting the interview as she did. The ability to think through how one should intervene, when in the midst of a complex interviewing situation such as this one, is a skill developed out of extensive experience. Careful study of the worker's questions and her parenthetical comments can be a valuable aid in understanding when and how one should intervene in a family interview, especially when tension grows and argu-

ments begin. Developing the ability to express clearly the rationale
for directing the interview in certain ways can help a counselor increase self-awareness of how her intervention may affect the interaction between and with family members.

    The Grant family was seen by the worker for approximately
nine months in a combination of family interviews, joint interviews
with Mr. and Mrs. Grant, and individual interviews. Two interviews
were held with Mark and Peter to work on the conflict between
them and to attempt to reestablish a basis for restoration of their
previous bond. This flexible approach to the unit of attention was
based on the diagnostic assessment that problems in the family had
to be addressed at multiple levels. Issues requiring a family therapy
approach were the issue of visitation by the father; the handling of
differences of opinion among family members; and adolescent developmental tasks of mastery related to identity and individuation in
the context of the remarried family's goals for closeness. On the
other hand, Mrs. Grant's response to her former husband stimulated anxiety in Mr. Grant and had the potential of becoming a
marital problem. During their joint sessions, Mr. Grant verbalized
his fears that his wife was still attached to her former husband and
his anxiety that this could break up the marriage. Work on residual
attachments was the focus in several joint sessions and in individual
sessions with Mrs. Grant.

    The boys' father was included in two of the family sessions,
after the work on the Grants' marital relationship had taken place.
The focus was limited to working out dependable visitation arrangements. The contact was an amicable one. It went far in reassuring
Mr. and Mrs. Grant that Mr. Stuart was able to accept the children's meaning to Mr. Grant as the stepfather, and that he felt this
was a gain for the children and would not want to disturb this
relationship.

    Ultimately, Mark agreed that he, too, wanted to see his father
on occasion as the conflict between the brothers on this issue was
diminished. A workable family balance was achieved in which the
father resumed weekly visits with Peter and visits with Mark when
Mark wanted them. As Peter felt more accepted for his decision,
and with the family's greater acceptance of his father, his surliness
was modified and he was able to engage more spontaneously with
family members. Throughout, it was necessary to clarify the complexity of the remarried family situation and to help the family accept the reality of the differences between a nuclear family and a
remarried family. At the same time, the Grants were helped to see

that the quality of family life need not be diminished because of these differences if appropriate goals were established, co-parenting roles with the nonresident father were worked out, and denial of differences was avoided.

24 Recapitulation

S ome recapitulation is now in order. In the light of our examination of the interviews presented and the illustrations they have furnished of our general discussion of salient characteristics of human psychology, we can review and summarize our suggestions on "how to conduct an interview."

Beginning

No matter how many questions have to be answered, no matter how much information he wishes to impart, the interviewer should always "begin where the client is." After making a brief introductory statement about the manifest purpose of the interview, it is usually most helpful if he asks a few leading questions that will enable the client to express what is on the "top" of his mind. Of course, the interviewer will have thought over the interview in advance and will know fairly definitely what he wants to obtain from it. But by letting his client talk first, he finds out the client's purpose and is able to pick up many leads for the best way of getting the information needed to help him. He knows his goals, but he will keep his plan of procedure flexible until such leads indicate the best course to take.

Somewhere during the interview, and often early, the client should be given a fairly clear idea of what the interviewer and his agency can do to help and of what kind of responsibility the client himself must assume in meeting his problem. Often the matter can be introduced by asking the client, "In what ways did you think we might be of help?" He needs reassurance that he has come to the right place for help, but he should not be overly reassured or led to feel that he is now relieved of all responsibility, that his problem will be "taken care of." Usually a very brief statement of the kind of services the agency tries to render will suffice at first. Later, as the interview proceeds, further explanation of the precise ways in which the agency can help can be given. Often an interviewer finds it useful in closing the interview to review with the client the next steps each has agreed to undertake.

Continuing

After the interviewee has told his story in his own way, the interviewer will make use of the clues thus revealed to introduce additional questions and discussion in crucial areas in order to fill out the picture and focus the interview on that territory that promises to be most fruitful for exploration. Expert direction of the interviewer is most called for at this stage. The interviewer must decide on the areas to be explored and the best way of drawing out the client. To elicit information successfully requires the establishment and development of the kind of rapport between the client and the interviewer that will give the client confidence in the interviewer's wish to help and in his having the understanding and knowledge required for effective assistance. Once this confidence has been established, the interviewer can carefully direct the conversation to obtain necessary information about the underlying basic factors of the client's specific problems.

It is not easy to achieve the golden mean of leaving the client free to talk spontaneously and at the same time giving the interview continued direction into fruitful channels. Mere listening and encouragement simply leave the client floundering in the same sea of uncertainty in which he was lost when he applied for help. But overdirection can stifle the interview in its infancy by preventing the salient features of the matter from rising to clear awareness.

Again, it is not easy to achieve the ideal balance between re lieving a client of the unbearable burden of what seem to him insurmountable difficulties and leaving him with essential responsibility for working out his own destiny. In the interviews we have considered, even when the client was most in need of help, the worker, through doing enough to make the difficulties seem conquerable, has in each case carefully left responsibility and initiative with the client. It is a temptation to work out a solution in full detail, especially when working with children or old people, but this temptation must be resolutely resisted. It is better to have the client feel that the plan is one he has been instrumental in developing and is carrying out, with help to be sure, but essentially on his own initiative, than to have all the details correct.

Closing

In bringing an interview to a close, several things should be kept in mind. It is usually a good plan to end with a recapitulation of "next steps." A tying together of the threads of the interview and a restatement of what interviewer and client are each going to attend to before their next conference are often valuable. If possible, a definite next appointment should be made. If the interview has involved considerable expression of emotion, the interviewer can usually avoid an emotional letdown by turning his client's attention to objective factors before closing the interview.

One of the most important skills for an interviewer is a knowledge of his own limitations. To know when to refer a client elsewhere, when to terminate an interview, when to explore an emotional situation, and when to leave some area unexplored requires skill that comes only with practice. He must not stop too soon or too late, but at just the right time. And "the right time" varies from person to person. With growing skill in interviewing, the timing is selected with increased ease and confidence. We realize that such skill cannot be acquired simply by reading a book, but a study of the theory of interviewing and thoughtful consideration of it in the light of one's own practice and experiences in interviewing will help a worker to develop his skill and render increasigly valuable service.